THE TROTTER WAY TO *Romance*

Nobody does it better!

ONLY FOOLS
AND HORSES

THE TROTTER WAY
TO
Romance

By Derek Trotter
As told to
John Haselden

BASED ON THE BBC TV SERIES BY

John Sullivan

WEIDENFELD AND NICOLSON
LONDON

Printed in Great Britain by Butler & Tanner Ltd,
Frome and London

Designed by Harry Green

PICTURE CREDITS Photographs (copyright BBC, licensed by BBC
Enterprises) were supplied by kind permission of the BBC
Photograph Library, except for the following: Hulton-Deutsch
Collection 8–9; Rex Features 61; Syndication International 13,
63br, 72, 73.

Contents

Acknowledgements
page 7

First Steps
page 9

Older Women
page 45

You Always Remember the First Time
page 79

Keeping it Together
page 105

Fateful Attraction
page 148

Acknowledgements

I am deeply indebted to all the birds who have passed through 127 Nelson Mandela House over the years and taught me about the problems and joys of committed relationships.

In particular, I would like to thank all of my fiancées, without whose enthusiastic willingness to assist in my research this book would not have been possible; Kirsty Ackland and Virginia Allan for being a constant source of inspiration; my brother Rodney who has contributed much material which should provide encouragement for my less fortunate readers; John Haselden for loyally pounding the keyboard once more; but most of all Raquel, for providing me with an heir to my business empire.

*C*rystal Palace 1951 ... The Trotter
Way to Romance is born.

First Steps

When my old mate Lord Widenfield phoned and said: 'Del, in *The Trotter Way to Millions* you shared with us the secrets of the board-room – how's about giving us the secrets of the bedroom?' I turned him down flat.

You see, what us yuppies call 'the realm of the cultural encounter' is populated by two kinds of punter: the doer and the talker. Those what do, do; those what don't, talk. And it's a well known fact that Del Trotter is definitely a doer. If I've said it once, I've said it a thousand times.

Threatening me with a large wallet, his Lordship said: 'Well, would your brother write the book for me?'

'No way, Pedro,' I said. 'Rodney writing a book on romance is like Oliver Reed carrying a liver donor's card.'

As us yuppies say: 'It just wouldn't have panned out.'

Finally, though, he did persuade me for posterity, the good of mankind and a cheque made out to 'cash'. You see, it's the principal that counts.

If you're going to go the distance on *The Trotter Way to Romance* it's no good being a talker. They just waffle on about their romantic lives but never actually get off the first tee. Let's face it, Rodney is a talker – and when there's a bird in tow he never *stops* talking, even when he's in bed. He learnt about long-term, committed relationships from *Wildlife on One*, so he can't do anything without a voice-over.

So one day I accidentally broke into Rodney's wardrobe and had a gander at some of his diaries. (Why does he lock his wardrobe? Don't he trust no one?) This short extract should show you what I'm getting at:

Friday

I go down the Nag's Head for a lunchtime pint. My problems with Bernice have put me in a rather philosophical mood. Trigger starts talking to me and I stumble on a great scientific discovery: It's impossible to be philosophical with a bloke who's a pork pie short of a picnic. I mean, for a start, he's got this idea my name's Dave!

'Anyway,' I venture, 'I said to her, I said: "Bernice ..."'

'That her name is it?' asks Trigger. I mean, what can you do?

'Yes, her name's Bernice. That's why I call her Bernice,' I say a bit sharpish.

'Right!' he says, as if he's discovered the law of gravity.

'I said: "Don't play with me, Bernice, 'cos you're playing with fire! Just don't try and tie me down!"'

'She's into all that is she?' asks Trig.

I want to walk out the pub then and there but I'm worried another rumour might start.

'No,' I explain calmly. 'I meant it in a sort of spiritual way! See, I'm a free agent, Trig. Wherever I lay my hat, that's my home. That's the type of guy I am.'

I take a swig of my lager while Trig ponders my last statement. I know he's trying hard to understand what I said. Then he comes back with:

'You got a hat now then Dave?'

It takes my breath away. I think, this is going to be a long day!

'No,' I explain, 'it's a saying.'

'I had a hat once!' he says.

'Really?' I say, not the least bit interested.

'someone nicked it at a party!'

I mean, bloody hell! There I am exploring the most turbulent regions of the emotional landscape and Trigger's talking about a knocked-off trilby!

I try to get us back onto the original track. 'Bernice was crying and begging me not to leave her...'

'Had my return train ticket in the brim!' replies Mastermind. 'I had to walk all the way home from Plumstead!'

'Good,' I say in a superior way. (I'm not an intellectual snob but some things just give me the hump.) Then in an attempt to change the subject, I order a toasted bacon sandwich.

'What colour was your hat, Dave?' says Trig. He just won't let go!

'Pink,' I say through gritted teeth.

'Same here!' he says.

I go to the toilet for half an hour. When I come out Trigger has gone - and my bacon sandwich is all cold and horrible.

Andrew Lloyd Webber could write a musical about Rodney's diaries – *The Plonker of the Opera*, something like that.

Romance. Blinding word, ain't it? Sort of – well, romantic! Down the ages poets and gurus and things have been asking the eternal question: What is it? And where can I get a bit?

Some scientists believe it's in the genes, and if they're talking about Rodney's Wranglers they're probably right. Others believe that you've either got it or you ain't, and in Trig's case I can't argue with that. But for the rest of you help is just around the corner. So stop pacing the floor like a caged lion that hasn't had a bit of wildebeest for months, and get stuck into *The Trotter Way to Romance*.

This book and how to use it

Equally at home on the bedside table or in the bottom of your executive aluminium briefcase, *The Trotter Way to Romance* guarantees hours of pleasure for beginners and experts alike. You can dip into it last thing at night, or first thing in the morning – whatever turns you on – but where better to start the ball rolling than:

The first step

The first step is The Pick Up. Some birds are very difficult to pick up; others are born with handles. Whatever, Rule Number One is: just make sure you're in the same room as her. But be aware – by the end of the evening you may be wishing you was in a different country to her. Take a short but sad tale Trigger recounted to us one time when we were comparing emotional scars. You'll realize he ain't called Trigger 'cos he's quick on the pull.

'I had a relationship break up a few years ago,' he said. 'She worked at my council depot.'

'What, a lady roadsweeper?' I asked.

'Oh no! She was management – real high-flier. You had to go to her when you wanted a new broom. Linda. Nice girl. Had a funny eye. Never knew if she

When Linda suggested a weekend in the country, Trig went off with the horse.

was looking at me or seeing if the bus was coming. Anyway, she heard about this little hotel out near Henley-on-Thames and she said to me: "How about spending a weekend there?"'

There was a long pause. Trig was momentarily lost in the mists of time.

'Well?' I said.

'Well what?' he said.

'Well . . . was it a nice weekend?'

Trigger rejoined the Planet Peckham. 'Yeah. Well, at least I thought it was . . . but she didn't wanna see me no more after it.'

'What happened?' I asked, my mind boggling.

'She got jealous,' he said. 'I heard later, through friends, that she wanted to go with me . . .'

I've heard of playing hard to get, but that was out of order! On the other hand, there are times when no 13 matter how much you beat them off, they just keep on coming. Before I settled down with Raquel Turner, I had so many birds after me they used to call Nelson Mandela House 'The Aviary'.

Playing hard to get

Whether you're a bird or a bloke you have to be very careful when playing hard to get. The timing of every move is crucial. Some of us, like *moi*, who have natural 'style' develop an instinct about these things. Others have to study hard and learn their lessons well.

I always kept to a regular pattern: every evening after a day's dealing I'd whip home to the Peckham penthouse, shower in Brut body gel, wash my hair with Timotei, slip into the cream Farahs, white loafers,

Rodney playing hard to get.

brown leatherette bomber jacket and all the tomfoolery, stick the Foster Grants on my barnet, pour a large Singapore Sling then settle down at the wrought iron effect, mock Georgian desk and sort out my social calendar. D'you see what I mean about *style?*

Then I'd hit one of the clubs – Annabelle's in Mayfair, Stringfellows in the West End or The Purple Pussycat in Brixton Hill. As you can imagine, with my style I never had to play hard to get. Women used to throw themselves at me. Covered in bruises I was. But Rodney – Rodney was different. He was one of the 'others'. He never had the instinct, the Force wasn't with him.

I remember one particular night, me and Rodders were having a quiet drink at the Purple Pussycat when this young sort sitting at the bar started showing out to Rodney. I assumed she must have been drunk but Rodney wouldn't have it. She smiled across at him and Rodney returned one of his sexy grins (well, he said it was a sexy grin; to me it looked like he'd just sucked a pickled onion).

'Go on, Rodders,' I said, 'get in there! Your luck's changed, bruv – ask her to have a dance.'

But Peckham's answer to Julio Inglassis said, 'I don't want her to think I'm eager. I'm going to play it cool.'

And he did play it cool. *Very* cool. I had to zip my jacket up at one point to keep warm. For the next hour or so this bird kept grinning across at Rodney like a synchronised swimmer but Julio was still playing hard to get. Then, just as they called last orders, Rodney made his move. Trouble was, so did six other blokes. She finally left the club on the arm of this good-looking scrap dealer from Deptford. Rodney still tried to chat her away from the bloke as they were leaving, but it was too little, too late. But he did learn a couple of valuable lessons that night:

LESSON 1: Don't waste time, even when you're playing hard to get.
LESSON 2: If you try to chat up a scrap metal dealer's bird you end up with a crumpled tie.

I tried to advise Rodney as best I could but, to be honest, it was out of my field of reference. The nearest I ever came to playing hard to get was taking my socks off slowly! Rodney put it down to bad luck, which was very wise of him, because as I will now demonstrate, luck is a very important element in the Trotter Way to Romance.

Strokes of luck

My fatal attraction plus a generous application of Brut lotion *après-rasage* (as they say in Biarritz) used to knock 'em bandy and there'd be some pretty heavy breathing before we reached my penthouse suite – usually because the lifts were out of order again. By the time they got up to the twelfth floor they'd be too cream-crackered to resist. And that's what I mean by luck! If those lifts had been working I could have had a load of goalless draws.

Those broken-down lifts came to the Trotter family's aid in other ways and almost got us the result of the century. It was during Rodney's Marxist era, which must have lasted all of six weeks. He used to go around in his Man at Oxfam suit and a Steve Bilko T-shirt spouting about equal rights and that sort of thing. Our old Grandad, Gawd bless him, was alive then and it used to drive him mad.

One evening I was standing by the mirror spraying my hair with Cossack when Rodney said, 'You've forgotten, ain't yer?'

'Forgotten what?' I said, and copped a mouthful of hair lacquer for my trouble.

'It's the monthly tenants' meeting tonight!' said Rodders in a voice that could have caused a strike at Dagenham.

I checked my social diary and he was right, I had forgotten the monthly tenants' meeting. I was choked! I'd really been looking forward to popping down to The Bernie Grant Community centre and sitting in a hall with four old codgers, a couple of winos who'd come in to get warm, and listening to speeches by Baz, the chairman of the tenants' association, who took umbrage at social injustice and key money from illegal immigrants.

'I'm sorry, bruv,' I said, 'but I'm going out with that little waitress from the Pizza Palace.'

A look of admiration filled his little face. 'How did you manage to get a date with her? She's almost the manageress!'

I smiled. 'Remember this, Rodders. RULE NUMBER ONE: Women are turned on by men in a position of power.'

'Yeah?' said Rodney, slightly bemused. 'So how did *you* manage to pull her?'

'I told her I was a Euro-minister!'

'And she believed you? Blimey, she must be thicker than them pizzas she dishes out.'

Rodney can be dead sardonic when he wants to be. I ignored his remark because I was in an optimistic mood, and also because it was true.

By now Rodney was on his soapbox, rambling on and on about the crime wave that had hit our estate. He produced a little red book and I remember thinking: Gawd, I hope he ain't going back to his Chairman Mao period – it used to give him eczema. But it turned out to be nothing more than a notebook.

*B*ut don't look a gift horse in the mouth

'I'm making out this catalogue of crime,' said Che Trotter. 'See what the Chairman of the Tenant's Association's got to say about that!'

I reckoned Baz might be making a few guest appearances in the catalogue himself, but Rodney had only managed one entry.

'May the Sixth,' I read. 'Grandad's shopping trolley was stolen from the pram sheds.'

I shook my head in disbelief bordering on despair. 'Gordon Bennett! There are two thousand stories in the Naked City and this plonker's looking for a basket on wheels!'

'But I need *facts*, Del! Times and dates. I've got to provide details, not rumours.' He was starting to sound like an arresting officer!

'Well, why don't you mention what happened to poor Rita Aldridge?' I suggested.

'Oh yeah! Cosmic!' said the man of the people, his pencil hovering over the page. 'What happened to Rita Aldridge then?'

'Last Friday night some geezer indecently assaulted her over by the adventure playgrounds.'

'By the adventure playgrounds?'

'Did she report it?' said Peckham's Conscience.

'Of course she did,' I said. 'I met her this morning. She'd just been down the police station.'

Rodney's eyes narrowed. At last he had a cause! Then he said: 'Hang on ... If this happened last Friday night, how come it's taken her to Wednesday to report it?'

'Because she didn't *know* she'd been indecently assaulted until this morning when the bloke's cheque bounced!'

Rodney can get very threatening with a pencil, so I thought it was as good a time as any to see what was on the menu at the Pizza Palace. It took me a while to realise that the broken lifts, Grandad's iffy legs and Rodney's socialism could be lucky omens. AND RULE NUMBER ONE OF THE TROTTER WAY TO ROMANCE: Sometimes even luck needs a nudge.

Positions of power

Rodney obviously took my line about telling birds I was a Euro-Minister to heart. When I saw him next morning he announced that not only had he attended last night's tenants' meeting, but he had also been elected as the new chairman.

Baz had resigned on personal grounds, pending the council enquiry. Trigger had proposed Rodders and Baz had seconded the motion. *Après moi le deluge*, as they say in Gdansk.

'Unanimous was it?' I asked.

'Only one voted against me,' Rodney said.

'Who was that?'

'Me! Baz and Trig voted in favour.'

18 'What about the others?' I enquired.

'There weren't any others,' said Rodney, his face reddening.

Okay, as elections go it might not have been in the same league as John F Kennedy's presidential campaign, but, like I always say: it don't matter whether you're in the boardroom or the bedroom, it only takes two to hokey cokey.

Involved as I was with silly little things like trying to make Trotters Independent Traders (TITCO plc) some profit whilst Chairman Rodney was away putting the world to rights, I suppose it took me longer than it should have to realise what was occurring. It wasn't until I caught him splashing some of my Eau de Yves St Dior *pour homme* over his Nike Panthers that I recognised the tell-tale signs: *There was a sort in the frame!*

The following week when he appeared in the market in a new suit from The Almost New shop I knew for certain that it wasn't just council business that was attracting him to the town hall every day.

'Where have you been, you dipstick?' I greeted him. 'I've been working my boots off in this market while you're swanning around in the corridors of power!'

'I had to see Miss Mackenzie.'

'Who's Miss Mackenzie,' I asked.

'She's in charge of housing and welfare at the town hall. She's a very important lady, *and* very impressed with yours truly. She's very intelligent – we get on really well.'

'Yeah, well, they say opposites attract,' I said. 'So that explains the new whistle?'

Rodney grinned that little shy boy grin of his. 'We've been seeing quite a lot of each other,' he said. 'I hope I wasn't too forward, Del, but today I asked if she would – well ... '

'Would what?' I asked, alarmed. I remembered the last time Rodders had asked a girl to do something. I'd ended up fighting her Dad.

Rodney said: 'I've asked her if she'd help me form a Police and local Community Action Comitee.'

RULE NUMBER ONE OF THE TROTTER WAY TO

19

ROMANCE: If you're ever dancing in a nightclub with an attractive person of the opposite sex – or whatever grabs you! – never ask if they'd like to form a Police and local Community Action Commitee. It didn't work for Rodney, it won't work for you. QED.

*M*ixing business with pleasure

I found myself thinking that if that was the only action Rodney was offering Miss Mackenzie, he might appreciate the Don Johnson of Peckham giving him a brisk canter along the Trotter Way to Romance. And, if called upon, I'd give her one as well.

I went into Grandad's bedroom later and told him all about Rodney and the bird from the town hall. In the Tescos of life Grandad was way past his sell-by date, but it did me good to watch a smile creep into his old eyes as he lay there in bed with his hat on. His legs had been really bad recently and he looked a tired old man. Our local GP, Doctor Becker, had recommended we apply to the council for ground floor accommodation and had told us about some brand new bungalows they had just built in Herrington Road. Now normally we wouldn't have stood a snow-ball's: you've got to have six kids and a prison record before the council will help you, and I didn't have any kids. But now, with Rodders strutting his stuff in the chambers of local government, it was a different story.

It may not surprise you to know that Rodney didn't immediately appreciate the beauty of my masterplan.

'I can't do that, Del!' he moaned. 'I mean, what would Miss Mackenzie think? I've only been chairman for a week and already I'm asking her for a new bungalow!'

'I don't care what she thinks. I'm only concerned with poor old Grandad.' I nodded towards his bedroom door. 'I mean look at the state of him. His mind went years ago. Now his legs have gone. There's only the middle bit of him left!'

'Couldn't we take him to Lourdes?' Rodney said.

'What's the good of taking him to Lourdes?' I said.

'He don't even like cricket.'

'No, Lourdes in France!'

'That's no good either. What we gained on the miracle cure we'd lose on the sea-sickness coming home.'

I realised, and not for the first time, that where Rodney's concerned it's always best if I take things into my own hands.

It took me another week to persuade Rodders to bring Miss Mackenzie up to the Think Tank of the Trotter empire for a dose of my *joie de vivre*. As I shook hands with her and ushered her into the boardroom I noticed there was already a flush in her cheeks. I put it down to chemistry. 'Don't they ever fix those lifts?' she said.

She must have been in her early thirties, and Rodney was obviously far too young for her – I mean, 21

a toy boy's one thing, but not when they come from
Fisher Price! She had a very nice figure and even the
House of Trotter couldn't have fitted her up with nicer
clothes. I know *designer cuisine* when I see it and this
was the full Monty.

*L*ateral chatting

'*Entendé*, I'm sure!' I said as I kissed her hand. 'Do sit
down, Miss Mackenzie. Can I get you some refresh-
ments – tea, coffee, a pina colada?'

She sank back into an armchair, breathless. Rodney
hovered in the background, slack-jawed with amaze-
ment. I can't say I blamed him. I was even surprising
myself. My charm was working like a stun-gun.

'No ... thank you ... that's very kind of you Mr
Trotter ... ' she gasped.

'*Mais oui, mais oui,*' I said. 'Call me Derek, please!'

'Derek . . . could I see your grandfather?'

I showed her into his room and gave it a quick squirt of AirWick Summer Breeze and then went off to mix myself a Manhattan. I felt a celebration was on the cards.

She returned about ten minutes later looking slightly bewildered. It was the effect my Grandad used to have on people.

'Still hanging on is he?' I asked.

'Your grandfather's a very interesting man, Derek. He was telling me how his own grandfather had died at the Battle of Rorke's Drift.'

'Well he wasn't *at* Rorkes Drift,' I explained. 'He was camped in a field behind it, but one night he went over to the Zulus to complain about all the noise.' I cracked up. Birds love a bit of a laugh and a joke, although this one stayed a bit quiet. I soon got the message. Miss Mackenzie was on the shy side. She needed some small talk to bring her out of her shell.

'Was it always your ambition to work for the council, Miss Mackenzie?' I asked.

Bingo! She relaxed immediately. 'Please, call me Margaret.'

'Margaret!' I said, marvelling at the music of the word. 'Do you know, that's my most favourite name.'

'Thank you.' Her eyes shone with gratitude. 'Actually, when I left school I wanted to be a choreographer.'

There was no stopping me now. 'Really? That's a coincidence, 'cos I often thought of going into the medical profession myself!'

Rodney cleared his throat. I'd almost forgotten he was still there. 'A choreographer, Del. She wanted to teach dance.'

'Oh *that* sort of choreographer!' I exclaimed. 'So you like dancing, eh, Margaret?'

'Well I was a student of dance for two years,' she said.

'No! So was I!' I said.

'Oh really?' she said. 'Where were you? I was at the London School of Dance, Knightsbridge.'

23

Rodney chose this of all moments to stick his oar in. 'Del was at the Arthur Murray School, Lewisham.'

I got the distinct impression he wasn't enjoying watching the master in action as much as he should have.

'Thank you Rodney,' I smiled. 'Now why don't you pop out the kitchen and stick your head in the food blender.'

I turned debonairly back to Miss Mackenzie.

'Do you like ballet, Margaret?'

I was right on the money.

'Oh yes,' she sighed. 'Very much.'

'Same here!' I said. 'Triffic, ain't it? What about that Nijinsky then?'

'Nijinsky?' she asked.

'Fabulous dancer, eh? Well, for a Soviet.'

'Yes. I suppose so.'

Knightsbridge or no Knightsbridge, I could see I was way ahead of her when it came to culture. I had to be careful not to get her confused.

'I'm a great fan,' I said.

'Of Nijinsky's?'

'Oh yes, can't get enough.' I unpeeled a Castella. 'In fact I've been thinking about getting a couple of tickets for one of the shows.'

'Derek,' she said quietly, 'Nijinsky died in 1950.'

I needed a bit of time to take this all on board. I gave my Castella a couple of good sucks and then wished I'd lit it.

'Did she?' I asked, dead casual.

'*She?* Nijinsky was a man!'

I mean, you can't reckon on something like that, can you? What sort of bloke goes round with a name like Nijinsky?

'Of course he was!' I said coolly. 'I always get him mixed up with . . . erm . . . ' I looked to Rodney, hoping he might throw me a cultural lifebelt.

'Arkle?' Rodney said helpfully.

All I've done for him and that's the thanks I get!

Miss Mackenzie packed her paperwork away in her briefcase and said: 'Well, that seems about it. I think I have all the information I need.'

'How long will we have to wait before we know if our application's been accepted?' Rodney asked.

'You can know right now Rodney.' She smiled. 'I've just signed it.'

'You mean we've got the new bungalow?' Rodders gasped.

'Of course. There's your new rent book and all the necessary forms.'

'I can't believe it!' Rodney was almost in tears and I felt very proud of him. 'Are you sure you wouldn't like to double-check it?' the little plonker said.

I had to act fast. 'Don't be silly Rodney,' I said. 'Margaret knows what she's doing!'

Rodney was gobsmacked. 'I just don't know what to say!'

'Just say thank you to the nice lady,' I said through clenched teeth.

Miss Mackenzie got up to leave. 'Really there's no need. I'm only too pleased to help. Many people get themselves voted on to tenants' committees purely for their own ends. But Rodney's different. He cares.'

I nodded vigorously and gave Rodders a cuddle. 'Oh yes, he cares. He's a forty-two carrot diamond, he really is!'

'Well,' she said, 'I hope you'll be very happy in your new home.'

Still nodding, I showed her to the door before Rodney had a chance to donate our new bungalow to a gay ecologists co-operative. Once I was alone with her in the hall I gave her the full voltage. 'I just wish there was some small way I could show my gratitude? But *Mon Dew* – why don't I take you out now and buy us both a celebratory drink?'

She gave me a smouldering look that seemed to say: I am Woman. 'Thank you,' she breathed, 'but I've got a lot of paperwork to finish.'

'Some other time,' I whispered, cool as a Bejam cucumber.

'Goodbye,' she said.

I placed a hand on her shoulder and gazed into her eyes. 'Not goodbye, Margaret. Let's just say – *bonjour!*'

It never fails. As the door closed behind her and I

went back into the lounge, I would have bet a pound to a penny that she'd be back for more.

Rodney was staring vacantly at the rent book. 'Well I've done it my son!' he said. 'That's the power of being Chairman, Del.'

Would you Adam and Eve it? Two weeks on the tenants' association and he thinks he's led a revolution! I had to put him right there and then.

'Leave it out,' I said. 'It was my old chat that swung the verdict for us.'

At that moment the bell rang, and set the seal on it. Margaret stood on the doorstep, obviously unable to resist my charms for another minute.

'Did you forget something?' I said.

She blushed again. 'Only my manners I'm sorry to say. I've just realised that you, quite naturally, would like to celebrate your new home. But as Rodney would have to stay in with Grandad you have no one to go with. So – if your invitation is still open . . . '

L'etat c'est moi! I was on a right result. 'Oh but of course, Margaret,' I said. 'Just give me *uno momento*.'

'I mustn't have too much to drink though,' she said. 'It goes straight to my head.'

'Really?' I grinned. 'I'll have to keep a close eye on you then, won't I? We'll just have time to catch a swift one down at the Nag's Head then I know this little all-night drinking club over New Cross.'

And with that I opened the door to the lounge to tell Rodders I was off out.

*B*ut can she take a joke?

Unfortunately Grandad, Gawd bless him, the dozy old git, chose that very moment to have a miracle. He appeared from his bedroom celebrating our good news with a glass of brandy in one hand, a cigar in the other, and singing and dancing to 'My Old Man Said Follow the Van.'

I've had some difficult moments in my time: which of us moguls hasn't? But I can't remember standing so close to a bird whose head was about to explode. And I can't honestly say I blamed her. Five minutes

*R*ule Number One of the Rodney Trotter Way to Romance: He Who Dan Dares, Wins.

ago Grandad had been laid out on his bed unable to wiggle his toes, now here he was doing an audition for Cats. The game was well and truly up. Me and my old fella had tried to pull a flanker – but all for a good cause!

'I am disgusted with the lot of you!' she shrieked. And she looked disgusted and all. Luckily enough Rodney, who knew nothing about our plan, was the first in the firing line.

'But especially with you Rodney. *I believed you!*'

'*I* believed me!' he said helplessly.

'I assume you'll be resigning, Mr Chairman?'

He nodded. 'First thing in the morning.'

She looked at us one by one. You could tell she wasn't pleased. 'I'm going to do you all yet another favour,' she said. 'I'm going to save you the incon-venience of moving! Good night to you all,' she said,

27

snatching the rent book from Rodney's trembling hands.

As she turned on her heels I said: 'Margaret – are we still on for that drink?'

I hate a bird without a decent sense of humour.

Compatibility

In the end, though, it all comes down to compatibility. Now I'm lucky on that score. I'm compatible with everyone – but there are some people who ain't compatible back. Don't get me wrong. I'm very particular when it comes to choosing who I share the last Tia Maria of the day with.

In later years Rodney became quite choosy as well. I suppose it was my influence. He's got a beautiful wife, Cassandra. They love each other very much and I'm keeping my fingers crossed their legal separation don't last too long.

On the beach: Wrong . . .   right . . .

*R*odney goes for the Gordon Gekko look.

When he was younger his naivety in the romance stakes used to show – it was quite embarrassing at times. His version of courtship was only a mating-call short of a *Survival Special*. Birds wouldn't go near him. That boy was blown out more times than a windsock. I don't know where he got to when God was handing out the Trotter Magic.

Rodney suffered. So did I. He was my brother. But who wants a brother who, when it comes to the opposite sex, has got his own personal five mile exclusion zone? In those days you could sit in the Nag's Head any night and hear tales of Rodney's latest failure with one sort or another. In the end I decided to stop doing it and help him instead.

Going for it

I don't know whether it was my words of encouragement or Uncle Albert singing 'I'm In the Mood For Love' at the pub piano that made him do it, but one Thursday night Rodney decided to make his stand. I was taking a few quid off Boycie and Trigger at the poker table as the landlord, Mike, went over to Rodney and his little mates. Mike was pulling his usual 'There are only two tickets left for the Saturday night pub disco' stunt.

'Rodney won't want *two* tickets, will he?' laughed Mickey Pearce.

This was like a red rag to a sheep as far as Rodders was concerned. 'What do you mean, I won't want two?'

'Well,' Mickey said, 'you won't be bringing a bird, will you?'

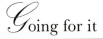

I've got to admit there were times when I thought Rodney was a fairy.

'Why shouldn't I bring a girl?'

'No reason Rodney, but why break the habit of a lifetime?'

Rodders drew himself up to his full height. 'I'll take the two Mike!'

'Who you bringing? Your Uncle Albert?'

'No. I'm bringing a girl.'

'Give over, Rodney!'

'*I'm bringing a girl!*'

'What's her name?'

I could see Rodney was having to think fast.

'Eh?'

'What's her name?' Mickey repeated.

'It's none of your business,' Rodney said. 'You'll find out on Saturday night, won't you!'

Mickey wouldn't leave it alone. 'Who is it? That sort from the fishmongers?'

'No it is not the sort from the fishmongers! This girl happens to be in ... er ... showbusiness!'

'Leave off!'

'I'm telling you the truth! You want to see her, she's a right bramma!'

Rodney's voice was taking on a strangulated quality. I left my cards and went to see if I could help.

'I've got ten says you won't bring a bird!' Mickey said.

We were in trouble.

'Why don't you make it twenty?' Rodney said.

Why didn't he take the entire TITCO annual profits and flush them down the khazi?

'What's all the noise about?' I said.

'He's betting me I ain't got a girl to bring to the do!'

'Well you ain't, have you,' I said reasonably.

'Yes I have,' Rodney said.

'Really?' I looked at him, then I looked at Mickey.

'Well take the mouthy little git!' I said.

'Right! Make it thirty, eh Mick?'

'Make it forty if you like!'

My blood was up. 'Go on Rodney,' I said. 'Go on my son!'

A silence fell across the bar. Even the smoke from

my Castella hung motionless in the air. Rodney's lips moved. It was only a matter of minutes before words started coming out.

'Why don't we make it a nice round fifty?' he said.

'You're on!' Mickey replied, laughing. 'I'll see you Saturday, and have your money ready.'

'He's got more front than Buckingham Palace, ain't he?' Rodney said when Mickey had gone. If I hadn't gone straight back to take some more of Boycie's money off him, I might have spotted him reaching for his tin of Barbican and trying to knock it back in one.

I noticed he was a bit down in the mouth as soon as we got back to the penthouse. 'Cheer up,' I said. 'Tomorrow's pay day, then Saturday night you take mouthy Mickey to the cleaners!'

There was a pause. Pauses always make me nervous. Pauses are what happen just before some tasty little sort says: 'I'm from the plain clothes division, have you got a receipt for that stereo?' or Rodney says: 'That's what's bothering me Del.'

'That's what's bothering me Del,' Rodney said.

I put a comforting arm round his shoulder. 'Now don't you start feeling sorry for Mickey Pearce. He's got too much old rabbit. Put him in his place once and for all!'

'Del-Boy' Rodney said slowly, 'I ain't got a girl for Saturday night. I ain't got a girl for any night!'

I stood back and looked at him, his little face all crumpled in defeat. It almost made me weep. This was a moment for gentle encouragement. I chose my words carefully. 'You stupid little plonker!' I said. 'Why did you keep upping the ante?'

'You told me to! You stood behind me going: "Go'n Rodders, go'n my son!"'

'That's because you said you had a date for Saturday and I believed you!'

'Well, I wasn't telling the complete truth!'

'Wasn't telling the comp ... ! You were lying through your back teeth, you mouthy little sod!' I turned to Albert. 'He stands to lose fifty on this!'

'Why'd you have to tell lies, Rodney?' Albert said. He took the words right out of my mouth. 33

RULE NUMBER ONE WHEN IT COMES TO ROMANCE: *Never* tell lies – unless it is absolutely necessary.

'It was pride talking!' Rodders squeaked. 'There was Mickey Pearce and some of the others laughing at me. So I pretended. Alright ... I lied!' There was a silence. 'Anyway, what's to say I won't meet a girl by Saturday night?'

What was to say Elvis Presley wasn't alive and well and living in the flat below?

'That's the spirit, Rodney!' Albert said. 'There's loads of girls on this estate. There must be *one* of them willing to go out with you.'

Rodney looked like a bulldog chewing a wasp. 'Well the thing is, Albert, I've been out with most of them in the past ... '

'What, didn't they like you?'

'Well they ain't formed a fan club yet, have they Rodney?' I said. I realised this was the moment to start trying to sort him out. It wasn't going to be easy, but I've always liked a challenge.

'I've got it!' I said. 'What about that tubby girl, lives over near the hall. She'll go out with you Rodney. She ain't the full deck!'

Rodney wasn't knocked out by the idea. 'I'll work this out myself if you don't mind, Derek.'

It didn't look too clever. Rodders had about as much chance of working it out himself as he would of taking over ICI. I mean, you can say a lot of things about my brother, but Lord Handsome he ain't.

'What about the barmaid from the Rose and Thistle?' Albert said. It wasn't a bad idea. Even Rodders could have had her on the slate.

He shook his head.

'I've cracked it, Rodney!' I said. 'Do you remember last month when I took you on that blind date?'

'Remember it?' Rodney exploded, 'I'm still having therapy for it! You're not honestly suggesting that I spend another evening with Big Brenda?'

There's no pleasing some people. 'Just 'cos she was taller than you! I've heard she's a very sporting girl!'

'Yes,' said Rodney. 'She was the Southern Areas shot putt champion!'

*R*ule Number One of The Trotter Way to Romance: Be Prepared. Here's Rodney preparing for a date with Big Brenda.

'You seemed to get on alright,' I said. 'You were moving around that dance floor like Wacko Jacko on speed!'

'Del,' he whined, 'I was frightened of her!'

*T*he little black book

I had a restless night, my dreams haunted by visions of Big Brenda rumbling towards me from one direction and fifty notes disappearing from the Trotter coffers in the other. There was only one thing for it. Del Trotter's Little Black Book.

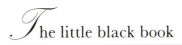

DEL TROTTER'S
<u>LITTLE BLACK BOOK</u>

The fact is, there's no substitute for a Little Black Book. I'm never without mine. It's my Bible, prayerbook and almanac. Since Raquel came into my life, of course, I've used it for reference purposes only, but I can remember a time when it meant even more to me than my old mucker Sir John Harvey Oswald's memoirs.

I've had more offers for it from publishers than you could shake a stick at. 'We'd update it every autumn, Del,' they all say. 'It'd be like the Good Food Guide, only tastier. This time next year you'll be a millionaire!'

Course, I never seriously considered it. Some things are sacred. Raquel thought so too.

'You'd have to publish posthumously, Trotter,' she said.

'Can't we at least talk about it?' I said.

'Of course,' said Raquel. 'Do you know a good medium?'

On the Friday evening I got out the Little Black Book as soon as I was back in the flat and phoned round some of my old girlfriends. It was twenty-four hours and counting, and Mission Control was in dead stuke unless it could pull something out of the hat. Sad to say, a fair number were no longer on the market. And at the mere mention of Rodney's name every single one of the rest either decided to wash her hair or felt a headache coming on.

'I tell you what, Uncle,' I said to Albert when I'd called the last on the list, 'phoning your old birds don't half make you feel your age!'

'Some of them married now, are they?'

'A couple of them are dead! Any messages while I was out?'

'Yeah,' he said. 'That young Mickey Pearce called, said he had the number of a lonely hearts club for Rodney.'

'Lairy little sod,' I said. 'I'd love to tuck him up, I
really would!'

36

*I*f the little black book
don't work . . .

. . . you can always try the Yellow Pages.

When Rodney emerged from his bedroom I realised that even the lonely hearts club was going to be a long shot. He was a real sight for sore eyes. He was wearing a white jacket, black trousers, a black shirt and a white tie. I tried not to react.

'Alright Rodney?' I said.

'Yep,' he said, heading for the settee.

I couldn't keep it up. 'Bloody hell! What have you done to yourself?'

'What you see before you is the new me! The old Rodney Trotter is dead. Long live the King!'

'You look like a liquorice allsort!' I said.

'You ain't got to wear it, have you?'

'Too true I ain't!' I said, thanking my lucky stars.

'I've got a few hours left to win that bet. I'm going out tonight, see if I can't bump into a right bramma!'

'Well just make sure you don't do it on a zebra crossing! I mean, with that gear it's now you see me, now you don't! Use your loaf, Rodders! How can you hope to pull a tart dressed up like Bertie Bassett?'

As ever, my advice fell on deaf ears.

'You ain't getting to me Del, so save your breath!'

'You know what would look good on you Rodney?' Albert said. 'A big white stetson!'

'You know what would look good on you Albert?' Rodney said. 'A doberman pincer!'

'Alright, alright,' I said. 'Take it easy, the two of you!' I looked at my watch, then asked Rodney if he wanted me to come with him.

'What are you going to wear?' he said, eyeing my market clothes.

'Sunglasses,' I said.

As I went off to change, Rodders had a sudden crisis of confidence.

'I don't think I'll bother, Del!'

'Come on,' I said, 'you've got to make an effort. He who dares wins!'

'That don't work for me Del. I'll just have to pay Mickey the money.'

I shook my head. Not since Norman de Trotter knocked the flaxen-haired maidens bandy at a cele-bration banquet after the Battle of Hastings had a member of our family failed to pull when it counted. But I could see the pressure was getting to him.

'I'll tell you what I'll do for you.' I produced a fiver. 'I'll buy that bet off you. If we win, I collect the fifty. If we lose, I pay out. How does that grab you?'

Rodney's eyes gleamed. He was as happy as Richard Gear in a pet shop.

'Good boy,' I said. 'You know it makes sense! Right, we're going to give them old dance halls a bit of an hammering tonight!'

'Yeah! Alright!' He paused. 'But Del, let's not just crash in there, kick them in the ankles and yell "Wanna dance darling!" Let's have a bit of decorum, eh? Bit of sophistication!'

What a nerve, I thought, as I gave myself a quick wash, a splash of Brut and selected a medallion or two. Sophistication was my middle name.

$\mathcal{O}$ut on the town

What a right blinding night it turned out to be. We went everywhere. The Empire Liecester Square, the Hammersmith Palais, you name it, we jived there – and the only thing I pulled was a ligament doing a bloody break dance.

We ended up in the Purple Pussycat at about three a.m. We'd checked out so many birds during the course of the evening I felt like I'd been through the qualifying rounds of Blind Date.

'Surely *one* of them girls would have done!' I said as we sat down.

'No they wouldn't Del,' Rodney said. 'This bird's got to be something special. I told Mickey she's in showbusiness.'

Some hope. The closest Rodney was going to get to showbusiness was Crufts. 'So where are we supposed to find a Bo Derek look-alike in Peckham at this hour in the morning?' I said. 'I mean, even Bo Diddley would be a long shot!'

'Well we're certainly not going to find her in this dump, are we Del? What did you bring us here for? Seems like a trouble place to me!'

He had a point. The Purple Pussycat wasn't the sort of joint I usually patronise. I used it occasionally when entertaining the sort of clients who weren't at home with pot plants and wrought iron table-legs. Rodney was glancing uneasily at the dried blood on the door handle, so I explained that their cleaner was off sick and attempted to focus his mind once more on our mission.

'What about them two over there?' I nodded in the direction of a table at the back of the club where a couple of tarts were doing their best to stay in the shadows.

'Do I look like St George?' he sneered. 'Come on Del, the blonde one's older than the Mary Rose!'

I shrugged. 'You said your girl was a film star. Bette Davis was a film star . . . '

'So was Rin Tin Tin!'

As I strolled over to the bar, I was forced to admit that in the bedroom, as in the boardroom, some things just can't be taught. At the end of the day, it don't matter how you dress, what you drink, where you go – it's that mystery ingredient that counts. Call it *servir frais mais non glacé*, call it killer instinct, you've either got it, or you ain't.

I glanced at my watch. Forty-eight carrots' worth of Patrick Phillipe. Nothing but the best. They don't make them like that anymore, not even in Singapore. Eleven forty-five, it said. It must have been about three-fifteen. Ah well, at least I could enjoy a final Pernod and ginger ale before saying bonjour to a bloody awful night.

The Trotter way to pull

I was on the point of hailing the barman when I bumped into Vonny. I used to see a lot of Vonny, and tonight was no exception. She was wearing a mini-dress that the House of Trotter catalogue would have advertised as a pair of pocket handkerchiefs. Vonny was that kind of bird. She never changed her style for nobody; what you saw was what you got. I'm always impressed by people like that.

*D*rinks: The Rodney Trotter Way. The Albert Trotter Way. The Right Way.

The only trouble was, when they assembled Vonny at the factory they'd spent much more time on the bodywork than they had on the in-flight computer. And as that thought danced nimbly across my mind I had a shrewd suspicion my problems were over.

'Watcher Vonny!' I said. 'How's it going?'

'Hello presh,' she said, leaning towards me in a way that said nothing much had changed. 'How are you?'

'Not too bad, darling. Doing a bit here and there. What about you, still stripping?'

She grinned. 'I'm not a stripper Del. I'm an exotic dancer!'

'Still take your clothes off though, don't you?'

'Well,' she said, 'it's part of the act!'

I told her I'd heard she'd been in a spot of bother a while back, and it all came tumbling out. A drug-crazed tourist had jumped up on stage and tried to strangle her. She'd been OK, luckily, but her snake was in bad shape. Since then, though, she'd got the sack from a lot of clubs for hitting the bottle.

'Doctor said I've got a drink problem, Del. I said I 41 ♥

ain't got a drink problem, I like it!' She raised her glass. 'Of course, my real problem is frustration ... '

'Can I help?' I asked, selfless to the last.

'I shouldn't be a stripper Del,' she said.

'Oh I don't know,' I said. 'I think it's a great idea!'

'Deep down inside I'm a singer! But no-one will take me seriously!'

I shook my head in disbelief. 'Gives you the hump, don't it!'

Unfortunately she chose that moment to sing the first couple of verses of 'I love you just the way you are' in my ear hole. It was like standing too close to a waste disposal unit.

'That's lovely Vonny,' I said, dead casual. 'You know, there's a do on at the Nag's Head tomorrow night. You fancy going?'

'Will they let me sing there?' she said.

'They'll insist,' I said.

'OK then,' she said brightly. 'You going to pick me up?'

'No,' I gestured behind me. 'You'll be going with my kid brother over there.'

She looked over my shoulder and frowned. 'There's no-one there. Just a geezer dressed up as a negative!'

'That's him,' I said. 'See, it's all to do with a bet. I stand to make fifty quid out of this!' I brought out my wad. 'Look, there's a score in it for yourself.'

I explained that she had to start the ball rolling by chatting him up, 'cos he had to believe it was for real. What follows is a short quiz. It is also a step-by-step guide to a: the Right (Trotter) Way to Romance, and b: what happens when you've got the wrong Trotter:

1. You are sitting on your own in an exclusive nighterie. You happen to glance at this very attractive sort sitting at the bar with everything on the counter. She smiles back. Do you:

a. Run your fingers casually through your chest hair, allowing her to see the glint of a medallion in the candlelight? Or

b. Look over your shoulder to see who she's looking at?

2. She picks up her drink, moves over to the spare chair at your table and asks: 'Is this anyone's seat?' Do you:

a. Run your tongue casually across your upper lip, grin and invite her to join you? Or

b. Say: 'Yes, I'm afraid it's my brother's'?

3. She sits. Up close the view is even more spectacular. She says: 'My name's Yvonne.' Do you reply:

a. 'I know. I've seen what you do with snakes'? Or:

b. 'I'm Rodne-cough-Rod ... Yeah, Rod ...'?

4. She says: 'I'm in showbusiness. I just called in here tonight on the off chance, I was hoping I might bump into some friends. I'd heard somebody was throwing a party tomorrow night. But now it looks as if I'll have to spend the evening on my own!' Do you:

a. Slide your ticket to the do at the Nag's across the table with a: '*Bonjour Trieste*, darling, it's your lucky night'? Or:

b. Imitate a man who's test-driving a new set of dentures and go: 'Yeah'?

――――――― · ―――――――

Score 2 for every answer 'a' and 0 for every answer 'b'. Give yourself 5 bonus points if you're wearing either a Bulgarian pin-stripe three-piece, white loafers and accessories or a rollneck and sheepskin with all the gold. Take off 5 if you're in a white jacket, black trousers, a black shirt and a white tie (unless you're going to a fancy dress party as a Belisha beacon).

If you scored:
- *−**5:** You are a plonker.*
  - ***0:** Give the do at the Nag's a miss this Saturday.*
  - ***5:** Either you're dressed right, or you can't count.*
  - ***10:** Congratulations my son. You're well on the Trotter Way to Romance.*
  - ***More than 15:** You're telling porkies. Only Michael Caine and Del Trotter have ever got more than 15.*

Actually, even Rodney took the hint after a while. When Vonny had said 'I've got absolutely nothing to do tomorrow night – there isn't a do at the Nag's Head by any chance is there?' a couple of times he got right down to it and asked her to join him.

Sadly, this particular stretch of the Trotter Way to Romance turned out to be a bit of a blind alley. Scarcely twenty-four hours later I found myself being pursued the whole way back from the pub by Rodney wearing a party hat and murder in his eyes.

'I ... am ... going ... to ... kill ... you!' he said between breaths.

'Come on Rodney,' I said reasonably once we were back home. 'Don't be a dipstick all your life!'

He wasn't at all happy. 'You put her up to it!'

I shook my head. 'I didn't. I paid her.'

'*Paid her?* That's even worse!'

I sighed deeply. Some people have no gratitude. 'I did it for *you*, Rodders, to save your pride. 'Course, I wanted to win the bet and all, but that was neither here nor there ... '

'*My pride?*' he bellowed. 'Tonight, in front of half of Peckham, the bird I told everyone was my girlfriend got up on the counter and took all of her clothes off!'

'I don't think anyone noticed though Rodney,' Albert said helpfully.

'Well you certainly did Uncle! You stood on a chair to get a better view!'

'Look,' I said, 'she had too many gins, that's all. I didn't know she had a drink problem!'

This didn't have the calming effect I'd hoped for.

'No,' Rodney said. 'I found out a lot of new things about her and all! Like I didn't know she could juggle light ale bottles, and I didn't know she couldn't sing – and where did that snake come from?'

'I don't know,' I said. 'No-one knows where it went either!'

What could I do? As I said at the beginning, it's all down to compatibility. I guess Rodders just wasn't ready for the kind of relationship Vonny was offering. I'm here to tell you he was the only one down the Nag's that night who wasn't, but there's no accounting for taste.

Well, even the Trotter Way to Romance don't always run true, though I never expected to lose money on the deal. To discover, after all my hard work, that Rodders had only bet Mickey fifty bloody *pence* in the first place was a right choker.

Older Women

For most people, the term 'Older Women' conjures up fantasies that most of you won't come across outside that Cynthia Pain movie. For Rodney it usually means anyone past their thirteenth birthday. Some of his dates used to arrive by skateboard.

Rodney's mates ain't fussy neither. They've always fancied themselves with anything in a skirt, as long as it's animal, vegetable or mineral and rigor mortis ain't totally set in.

I once watched, spellbound, as Jevon and Mickey Pearce failed to impress a couple of thirty-five year-olds.

'Jevon,' Mickey said, 'I spy with my little eye two women of the more mature variety.'

'Lonely housewives out on the pull,' Jevon said.

'I know you from somewhere, don't I?' he said, when he got good and close.

'I wouldn't have thought so,' the tastiest one replied, looking like she'd just trodden in something.

'He never forgets a face,' Mickey said.

'Neither do I, and I'd certainly remember you two!'

'Did you go to the Dockside Junior School?' Jevon said.

'Certainly not!'

'Told you!' Mickey said to Jevon. Then he turned to the bird.

'He thought you was our old headmistress!'

I'd be the first to admit that I've knocked around with a few older sorts myself in my time – it's how I learned so much about antiques!

I remember one in particular, a bird who worked in the local pie'n'mash shop, and to save Ursula Mimms from embarrassment I will refer to her as Miss X. Poor girl, she was getting on a bit. They said that in the war she'd had more Yanks than Eisenhower. Anyway, the thing about Miss X was, she was one of them what like to do the bizzo to music. It all started off very romantic. We used to go round to her house of a Wednesday afternoon when the pie shop had early closing.

*R*omance can make for some strange bedfellows.

Then one day she said to me: 'I'd like to make love while John Williams plays the guitar.'

I said: 'Leave it out, Ursula. Let's put a record on instead.'

I mean, I don't want some Welsh voyeur blimping me while I'm involved. There's no telling where it'll lead to; we could have ended up with the Shadows at the foot of the bed.

Now Rodney's different. He wouldn't have minded if the Gypsy Kings were standing on the ottoman playing Volaire. I sent him off once to collect a bit of weekly that was in arrears and he came back and announced he'd fallen in love with an older woman. I wasn't much the wiser – I mean, older in his terms could have meant anything from a first former in Grange Hill to a senior Brownie.

'Oh, he's fallen in love with someone who's got the vote this time!' I said to Grandad. 'How old is she – twenty?'

'No,' he said. 'She's about – thirty.'

'What do you mean about thirty?' I asked him. 'How old is she exactly?'

'Forty.'

'Forty? You're not serious are you?' I said.

Don't get me wrong, there's nothing unusual about going out with a woman of forty. Nothing, that is, if you happen to be fifty! I mean, this Irene sort was too old for me! Even Grandad would have to think twice! When she was drinking frothy coffee with some Ted up the Lyceum, Rodney was still struggling to keep gripe water down. I could hear Mum turning in her grave at the very thought of it.

'Course, Rodney never does anything by halves. He couldn't be content with just picking up a bird who watched the Golden Girls and wondered what the young generation was coming to. No, Rodney had to pick one who also happened to have a husband. The only silver lining that I could see, apart from her hairdo, was that at least the husband was away. But then Rodney told me where.

Parkhurst!

Seems he had a little bit of a temper, too. He was 47

in for wounding with intent, GBH, and attempted murder. Not for very much longer, though. He was being released soon.

'When he's out, Del,' Rodney asked, 'do you think I should go and see him, explain about me and Irene, man to man?'

'Well let me put it this way,' I said. 'If one day you find that you're really fed up with having knees in the middle of your legs, then do that. If, on the other hand, you've grown attached to them, emigrate to Vietnam.'

The stupid little plonker! What did he think this was, Jackanory? This bloke was a killer! Come to think of it, one set of kneecaps might not be enough for him. This whole thing could turn into a family vendetta.

Rodney still couldn't see the problem.

'He only got done for *attempted* murder,' he said.

'Maybe that was a bit of practice,' I said. 'You could be his first big success!'

'You're just like the rest of modern society,' Rodney said. 'Frightened. Well I've got a life to live and I'm not having a mindless thug like her old man, Tommy Mackay, telling me what I can and what I can't do! This is a battle I'm going to have to win.'

What was he planning to do – carry tins of spinach around with him? Still, he'd asked for my advice and I gave it to him. I give it to you all. Either steer clear of birds with big, bad husbands, or learn to sleep with one eye open. If not, I hope you enjoy wearing concrete overcoats and propping up the M26. And if you find that you still can't leave well alone, I just hope that you've got a big brother like me.

With Rodney I had to go right back to basics.

The end of the affair

A few days after his shock announcement, God's gift to senior citizens was sitting nursing a scotch in the Nag's. He'd had a bit of a kick in the stomach, poor boy. Not from Tommy Mackay, but from life. Irene had finished with him.

'Well, all's well that ends well I suppose,' I said philosophically.

Rodney shot me a glance in return that I have to say didn't look too philosophical.

'Come on now,' I said, putting my arm around his shoulder. 'Look at it like this. You've had a good time, a few drinks, little bit of humpty dumpty, and now it's finished.'

'You're a pig, ain't you!' Rodney snapped. 'That is the pinnacle of your aesthetic appreciation, ain't it – a few drinks and a bit of humpty dumpty!'

I chose to ignore this little outburst. I could understand how he felt. Irene had given him the push, and Rodney had to seek a new romance. And with his track record, that might not be till round about the time of Haley's Comet's next visit.

Still, there's no doubt it was all for the best in the long run. I knew what would have happened. One

day he'd have gone down the roller disco and met some blinding eighteen year old sort who'd have knocked his eyes out. And knowing how coordinated Rodney was on a pair of rollerskates, he would probably have knocked *her* eyes out and all. Then he would have had to break the news to Irene. How did he think a forty year-old woman would feel, losing in love to a younger woman?

'And she wouldn't be losing just any man,' I said. 'She'd be losing *you*, Rodney! That scar would never heal. So, *che sara, sarah* as the French say. Anyway, her old man was released yesterday, so you've been saved from all that.'

Rodney brooded a while into his scotch, then slowly nodded his head in agreement.

'The emotions that you have been experiencing are what separates you from morons like them punks over there,' I said, pointing at the group of scruffs who were playing Space Invaders in the corner only without the machine. 'You have proved that you are a human being, in the fullest sense of the word,' I went on. 'You have a heart, Rodney, and those feelings deserve respect and dignity. Don't feel ashamed of them – feel proud!'

As I left him to ponder the significance and poignancy of my words, I went up to Julie at the bar and ordered more drinks.

'What's up with him?' she asked.

'Oh, some old tart gave him the sack,' I winked, 'you know what he's like!'

Rodney got the first sniff of something fishy when Irene's son Marcus, one of the punks in the corner, walked past our table and said, 'Watcher Del.'

I could almost feel the cogs grinding into action in Rodney's brain. Ten minutes or so later he fixed me with a quizzical look.

'How did you know Irene's husband had been released?' he asked.

'You said,' I lied.

'And how did Marcus know your name?' he pressed home his advantage.

'Look, I'm wearing a medallion with a big D, ain't I?' I said, feeling distinctly edgy. 'It's obvious my name is Del!'

Somehow I just knew that not even Rodney would let me get away with that one.

'Marcus!' Rodney called out across the pub. 'How did you know my brother's name?'

'I met him last Thursday when he took my Mum out for a drink,' Marcus replied helpfully.

'I did it for you, Rodney!' I got in quick. 'I mean, do you want to end up dead?'

'No,' he spat. 'But it's nice to have the choice!'

The pain of separation

I'm going to draw a veil over what happened next, because it's a bit of a painful episode. It certainly rammed home to me the agony and violence that a broken relationship can bring in its wake.

To cut a long story short, Tommy Mackay, three of his mates, and a couple of baseball bats bumped into me later that night in the alleyway behind the Star of Bengal. Tommy thought that I was Rodney, and so did the baseball bats.

When I came to, I was faced with a long, painful limp back to the Nag's, and an even more painful dry cleaning bill.

'I fell down the stairs in Monkey Harris's house,' I muttered to Rodney by way of explanation.

'He lives in a bungalow,' Rodney said.

'Listen, Rodders,' I went on, my voice thick with emotion and splinters, 'I had a bit of a chat with Tommy tonight, and guess what? He's seen the error of his ways! I've cleared the path for you and Irene!'

'Me and Irene?' Rodney looked aghast. 'Oh no, that's all over, Del!'

'What?' My heart sank.

'We had a long talk about it,' he explained. 'We both realised it would never work.'

'It will work, Rodney!' I said. 'There's a box of Black Magic in the van, I've only had one out of it. Whip 'em round to her a bit lively!'

'It's no good, Del. It was just circumstances that threw us together. She was lonely and in a strange part of town, and I was just looking for a mother figure. You were right, Del!'

For once in my life, I wished that I wasn't. I would have sobbed with frustration, except my ribs hurt too much.

'You were right about something else and all, Del,' Rodney grinned.

What this time? I couldn't bear it.

'I went down the roller disco this afternoon,' he said. 'I met this bird, Zoe ... Eighteen, with a body that makes Madonna look a cert for plastic surgery! Irene was infatuation, Del, but this is love!'

Zoe rollerskated back from the Ladies and Rodney introduced her to me.

'This is my brother Del,' he said, getting up to leave. 'He fell down some stairs.'

'Hey, Del!' Rodney called back over his shoulder as they reached the door. 'I'd get that head looked at if I was you!'

They was the truest bloody words he'd ever said. Even so, I still believe:

A little white lie never hurt anyone

Be true to yourself at all times – that's what Mum always used to tell me and that's what I've brought up Rodney to believe. There are one or two exceptions, of course, like when a bird turns up on your doorstep with a rather rounded belly and you have to come clean and tell her you have a certificate to prove you've been sterile since birth, or when you receive a letter from the Inland Revenue addressed to Trotter & Son, Independent Traders and you find it necessary to write 'Moved To' on the envelope and add an address in Cocabanana.

For Rodney, however, everything that happens in life seems to be an exception, with the result that he tends to end up telling porkies a bit too often for his own good. What follows is an object lesson in how not to be true to yourself on a date, and thereby not only betray your conscience and most deepest held principles, but also to end up getting a blank. My source of information, you won't be surprised to hear, is Rodney's diary:

Got a date with Nerys, the barmaid at the Nag's.
'I was wondering if you'd like to go out somewhere in the week?' I ask her casually yet firmly, sort of Tom Cruise fashion.
'Where?' she asks.
'I don't know, anywhere,' I say, jawing a wad of gum and adjusting my aviator sunglasses.
'Who with?' she goes.
'Me.'
'Yeah, all right then.'

*S*mall talk was never Rodney's strong suit.

$\mathscr{P}$eckham's Top Gun.

So far so good, but young Maverick, Peckham's Top Gun, was not scanning the sky for bogies like he should have been. Jevon and Mickey Pearce came at him from out of the sun:

'I'll bet you didn't get a date with her!' Jevon says.
'Save your money, Jevon my man,' I go, 'I'm taking her out next week.'
'How'd you manage that?' he asks, clearly astounded by my technique. 'I've been trying to date her for ages – and bear in mind who's talking here. I've had to employ a secretary to handle all my dates!'

'Rodney's got something you haven't got, Jevon,' says Mickey. 'It's a thing called machismo! I've told you before, Nerys is turned on by macho-men!'

This was interesting news. I made a note to go a bit more on the Schwarzenegger on our date.

'And I've known Rodney longer than you,' Mickey says, 'and when he wants to be he's a real hard nut.'

You can say one thing for Mickey Pearce. He knows his mates inside out.

'Yep, that is what Nerys goes for,' he adds. 'Muscle and sweat.'

'Yeah,' Jevon goes, 'but Rodney's no master of the universe.'

'But he has the aura of inner strength,' Mickey says.

'I'm wirey, see,' I say modestly.

'Nerys likes guys who live their lives at a hundred miles an hour,' Mickey goes on. 'And they reckon when she's hot she is hot! The only guy who could put her out is Red Adair and he's too expensive.'

'Well I think you should treat a chick with consideration,' says Jevon, obviously pretty jealous that Nerys has gone for my muscle, sweat and machismo.

'And that's why you'll never get a date with Nerys,' Mickey says to Jevon. 'She prefers a bunch of fives to a bunch of flowers. But if my main man here plays his cards right...'

'Hey!' I give him five.

Romance in the fast lane

Rodney put on his most macho-est gear for his date with Nerys – dirty jeans with a large silver-buckled belt, a T-shirt that was just like his mind – grubby and armless – and a thick leather wrist band. He hadn't shaved for a couple of days, and his hair was 55 greased back. What a sight! He couldn't have pulled a bag-lady in that lot, let alone dear little Nerys.

'I thought you were taking that Nerys bird out?' I said.

'I am,' he said.

'Well you'd better get ready or you'll be late.'

'I am ready!' said Mad Max.

'You're going out like that?' I couldn't believe it. Had so many years of advice from the master really all disappeared down the waste disposal?

'What's wrong with me?' he asked.

'You look like a hooligan,' I said.

'It's the fashion,' he sneered. 'Haven't you read about it? It's called the James Dean look.'

'Yes,' I said. 'But when they say the James Dean look they mean *before* the crash! I can't see you getting very far with young Nerys dressed like that, Rodney.'

'Will you just keep it out,' he tapped his nose, 'and let me lead my own life!'

'I won't say another word,' I said. ' Maybe she goes for blokes who look like Barney Rubble.'

Uncle Albert wandered through the lounge on his way to the launderette.

'I thought you were going out?' he said.

'I am going out,' Rodney said crossly.

'Well hurry up and change,' Albert said. 'I'll take those clothes down the launderette for you.'

'I'm wearing these clothes!' Rodders snarled. He had his wild up now, good and proper.

'Yeah?' Albert chuckled. 'Where you taking her then, scrumping?'

I pick up Nerys in the three-wheeler and seem to be making a bit of an impression. Until, that is, I coolly take the roll-up from between my lips and flick it out of the window. The fag hits the glass, which I have forgotten to wind down. We have to bale out a bit lively.

We then experience a bit of a fracas with a Cortina load of yobs that cuts me up at a T junction. But I just give them the finger, Marlon Brando fashion, and shout, 'Swivel on that, camel-breath.'

Nerys seems quietly impressed.

'I always thought you were such a quiet person,' she says.

'They're the ones you've gotta watch, Nerys,' I say. 'I've lived in these streets too long to be frightened. Those punks back there are used to people running scared from them. But they don't scare me, Nerys. This is my jungle, and I'm at the top of the tree.'

I am feeling pretty confident, too, until I look in the wing mirror and see that the Cortina has turned around and is right behind us. With a great crunch of gears I hurl the van into third gear and we're away.

'Why are we going so fast?' Nerys asks.

'I love speed,' I say.

'You said we were going to cruise!'

'Yeah, but I like to cruise quickly.'

We race over the brow of a hill, smoke belching from the exhaust. It's like a remake of Bullitt, only this time it's down Lewisham Hill. At the bottom is a set of traffic lights, and they turn to amber when I am about a hundred yards away. I put my foot down in an attempt to beat the lights but they turn red. There's nothing for it. I put my life in the hand of the gods. The other traffic begins to move forward. I shut my eyes and listen to the symphony of screaming tyres, blaring horns and breaking glass. When I open them again I expect to find that I am in Heaven, but in fact I am going down Herrington Road past the Star of Bengal. In my rearview mirror I just have time to see what looks suspiciously like a police panda car which has crashed into the back of another vehicle. Nerys sobs uncontrollably. I think James Dean can safely assume that tonight he will be Rebel Without A Bit.

*R*EBEL WITHOUT A BIT.

Which just goes to show that one of the biggest questions on the Way to Romance will always be:

What motor?

It's a known fact amongst us world class moguls that Britain's future lies fairly and squarely in the second-hand car trade. It also won't have escaped your attention that there's nothing quite like a decent set of wheels for pulling the birds. Cushty, ain't it? Buy yourself a used motor (the chances are Trotter Independent Traders will have just the model for you) and bingo – you're putting the balance of payments to rights, *and* you're on a result!

'Course, you've got to make sure you invest in a tart trap rather than a death trap, and if you're new to the game it ain't always easy to tell the difference. As

a general rule, the first is for pleasure and the second is strictly business – but don't worry, we all make mistakes in the early stages, and if you should find yourself in possession of an old black Mark 2 Zephyr convertible with bald tyres, rust spots and no brakes, you'll follow my advice and flog it to an Australian at the first available opportunity.

We found ourselves gazing in wonder at just such a machine in Boycie's yard, way back when Rodders was just out of short trousers.

'It came in with a Chesterfield and a gross of electric toothbrushes as a part-chop on a Vanden Plas,' Boycie explained with uncharacteristic honesty. 'Still,' he said, as Rodney eased himself in behind the wheel, 'clean it up, couple of new tyres!'

'Yeah,' I said. 'New body, new engine, could be a nice little motor.'

'Well what would you like for fifty quid?'

'That's very nice of you Boycie,' I said, pointing at an open-top E-Type with white-wall tyres sitting on the edge of the forecourt. 'I'll take that ... '

'You would as well wouldn't you?' Boycie said, as we walked across to it. 'Only E-Type Jags and Sebastian Coe make me proud to be British these days!'*

'I know just what you mean Boycie,' I said. 'Why don't you put this little beauty on the front?'

'It's not for sale mate. I've bought it as a birthday present. I'm trying to find somewhere to hide it for a week; I'm frightened stiff the wife's going to see it before the big day.'

'What, and spoil the surprise?' Rodney said.

'It would spoil everything Rodney,' Boycie said. 'It's a birthday present for my bit on the side!'

The old software started to warm up at this point, and I began to see how we could knock off two birds with one stone. Or more if we played our cards right.

'*Mon Dew*,' I exclaimed, 'of course! You want to hide this for a week? Well we've got an empty garage round on the estate. I'll pop it in there if you like.'

Without the right set of wheels you're nowhere.

---

* Time flies, don't it?

Boycie's eyes glinted. 'Be handy, Del Boy. Might save me a lot of aggro ... ' Suddenly, his mind was made up. 'Right, I owe you one Del.'

'Don't be silly Boycie,' I said. 'It's a fine thing when you can't do a pal a favour without expecting something in return!' I paused, then looked over towards the Zephyr. 'How much did you want for that again?'

I turned back the speedo from ninety-eight to twenty-three thousand and took out the oil warning light bulb so it didn't stay on all the time. It did the trick. I flogged it to an Aussie for £199 the same day. I didn't mention that with those brakes the only thing he'd pick up in it was kangaroos.

I don't think Rodney approved, but it was around then that he was spending a lot of time in his room pining for Monica, that little fat bird, so I couldn't tell.

'I dreamed I was drowning last night!' he'd said to me that morning.

'You make my teeth itch Rodney,' I'd said. 'When you're getting your end away the skies are blue, the lager's cool and England are going to win the World Cup. Then some little tart with fat thighs gives you the elbow and it's worse than a visit from the VAT man!'

'She has not given me the elbow!' he insisted. 'Monica and I were having problems getting it all together on a one to one basis. So Mickey Pearce – he's lived with a woman – advised us to have a two week trial separation.'

Now I'm not against trial separations. I've always said abstinence makes the heart grow fonder. But a two week separation when you've only known a bird two weeks is stretching a point. I told him so.

'A fortnight on, a fortnight off? What is this, sentry duty?'

'There are plenty of other chicks Del,' he said.

'The way you're going your best bet is a blind date with a Samaritan!'

'I'll survive, Del Boy,' he said, sighing.

'So will she,' I said to cheer him up. 'I saw her last night at the Nag's Head disco, bopping away with your mate Mickey Pearce!'

This didn't seem to go down at all well. The evening of our visit to Boycie he suddenly appeared wearing a black suit, white shirt and slim Jim tie.

'You going to a funeral?' I said.

'No,' he said. 'I'm going to do what Monica was doing last night.'

I frowned. 'You're going dancing with Mickey Pearce?'

'No. I'm going to paint the town red; rip it up a bit. I'm going to hit a few clubs up West.'

'You'd need a compass to find it,' I said.

'I'm often up West,' he spluttered. 'I'm one of the faces!' There was a lengthy silence. 'Er, fancy tagging along Del?'

*R*odney and his mates going for a night up West.

'Not really,' I said. 'But if you're hard up for a bit of company I'll come.'

'Me? Hard up for company?' he said. 'You must be joking. I've got hundreds of friends!'

'Good,' I said, reaching for the paper.

'There's the cats from the evening school for a start!'

'Cats?' Grandad said, momentarily distracted from the TV. 'Where you going Rodney, dancing or ratting?'

Poor old Rodders hung around the front door for a while saying things like: 'We have lift off!' and: 'Right, I'll be off then!' then: 'Well, when the going gets tough, the tough get going!' without actually moving.

Finally I took pity on him. Another quick spin up the Trotter Way to Romance was clearly necessary.

'Right,' I said. 'I've got the money, the keys to the van – what are we waiting for?'

Rodney hesitated. 'We're not driving up West in a three-wheeled van, are we?'

'Well I'm not bloody walking it!' I said.

'But it's all about images, ain't it Del. I mean, you're very suave and debonair ...'

This took me by surprise. It looked like he was taking some of my lessons on board after all.

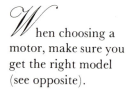

When choosing a motor, make sure you get the right model (see opposite).

'Well, yes, I suppose I am a bit ostentatious,' I admitted modestly.

'Exactly. Still, if I take the wheel and you hide down behind the dashboard, no-one will see you arrive.'

'I want people to see me arrive!'

'In a three-wheeled van?' he said. 'Oh well, I suppose we've got no choice, have we?'

Choice? Del Trotter always has a choice. 'Yes we have,' I said. 'We'll take Boycie's Jag.'

When not to take the van

There are some nights when even the Trotter magic takes a while to make its presence felt, but then again, seven-thirty is a bit early to go clubbing, even in an E-Type Jag.

The first place we went to was so dark it could have been used by a coal miners convention, only tonight they were all on strike. Apart from a couple of sorts by the bar there was only us and the waiter. I called to him through the gloom.

'*Garcon, la petit pois!*'

He was very pleased to see me. '*Parlez vous Français?*' he asked.

'*Jawohl!*' I said, putting him at his ease.

'What can I get you?'

'I'd like a Caribbean Stallion,' I said.

'Wouldn't we all, dear!' He seemed quite excited by the idea, until I explained that it was a drink.

'Write this down,' I said.

Take one shot of Tequila, one of coconut rum and one of crème de Menthe.
Add a smidgin of Campari and a mere suggestion of Angustura bitters.
Top it up with fresh grapefruit juice, shake — do not stir — then slowly pour over broken ice.
Garnish with slices of orange, lime and seasonal fruit, add a decorative plastic umbrella and two translucent straws and — voilà!

That recipe has been handed down in the Trotter family from generation to generation, ever since Roger Moore drank one in Live And Let Die. But beware! It should come with a Government Health Warning.

'Del,' Rodney said when the waiter had gone to fetch our drinks, 'do you think Monica was two-timing me all along?'

''Course not!' I said reassuringly. 'I mean, if she'd had someone else to go out with she wouldn't have wasted her time with you, would she?'

He spent a bit of time thinking this through.

'She thought I was weird!' he said. 'Well, not so much weird, more ... warped ... '

I went very still. 'Why?'

He had that very intense look he always gets when he's pondering the mysteries of the universe. 'Well, it's just ... Let me ask you this, Del. Have you ever had a fantasy?'

'Me?' I said. 'Never!'

'Yes you have!' he said. 'You go to bed at night and dream about Martini adverts! You've told me about them. You see us driving through St Moritz in a Ferrari Dino, two birds in the back – Gabrielle and Bianca – bra-less but class! We pull into a mountainside bar, just above the Cresta Run, where we don our Gucci ski glasses and drink red drinks all day without getting legless!'

'That's not a fantasy,' I explained. 'That's an ambition!'

'Same thing,' he said. 'Well I had a little fantasy of my own ... Uniforms turn me on!'

Don't get the wrong idea about Rodney. It wasn't postmen's or gas-meter readers' uniforms! He might be a pervo but he ain't dangerous. It was women's uniforms, but all the same this thing wasn't exactly what psychiatrists would call 'normal'. Apparently it started that time he got nicked in Basingstoke. He noticed the swish of nyloned thigh upon nyloned thigh, the squeak of rubber soles on parquet flooring as two policewomen escorted him into the station. The trouble with Monica started when he tried to get her to wear one. He'd tried to do it without her twigging.

'I was going to do it gradually,' he said, 'over a period of time. Last week was her birthday so I bought her one of those blue serge suits that Paddy the Greek was selling. I got her a hat, white with a navy blue peak ... Then for Valentine's Day I was going to buy her some black stockings and a pair of sensible walking brogues ... '

Christmas would have been a right wow – a pair of handcuffs and a whistle. It was lucky she packed it in before he had to fork out for a panda car. And talking of packing it in, it was about then that I decided we ought to. Our drinks cost the best part of a tenner, the two birds at the bar turned out to be geezers and I was about to get Chapter Two of *I, Rodney*.

The best use of the key ring

Fortunately the next joint we chose turned out to be a winner. After my close encounter with the dustmen in drag I thought with our luck we'd be spending the night with Hinge and Bracket. But no sooner had we paid the membership fee than the Trotter radar picked up the fact that this was a target rich environment. We zeroed in on a couple of super-league sorts at a corner table. What follows is a series of classic Trotter moves that all students of romance should do their best to memorise:

1. Saunter over, making absolutely sure they've got lumps in all the right places.
2. Accidentally drop your E-Type Jag keys on their table.
3. Go: 'Whoops! Dropped the keys to the E-Type Jaguar, metallic aubergine, white-wall tyres, ninety in third!'
4. If you have a brother or even a friend called Rodney, try this refinement: 'Actually, it's not my car, it's his!'
5. When he says: 'Eh? Oh! Yeah, er, it's my car!' you follow with: ''Course, we're only using it while they service my Ferrari.'
6. Sit down and introduce yourself, something along

the lines of: 'Hi! I'm Del – short for Derek. It's a nice name, Derek, don't you think?'

7. Couple of drinks and a bit of chat and you're on a result.

There are variations. Rodney still favours the lengthy pause followed by: 'Do you come here often?' as an opener, but that has the same effect as a nice sharp razor blade and a warm bath to a Roman.

I'd recommend 'We're on the international professional tennis circuit' as an alternative, and it worked a treat that time.

The birds were called Nicky and Michelle, and they were cut glass I can tell you. I nodded at Rodney and said: 'He's an international professional tennis player and I'm his manager. You must have heard of Rodney; the sporting press call him Hot Rod!'

'I can't say I have,' said Nicky. 'What's the surname?'

'Trotter!' said Rodney.

'Doesn't ring a bell, sorry.'

'Not surprising,' I said. 'We do tend to concentrate on the big American tournaments.'

'Do you ever play Wimbledon?' Michelle asked.

'No,' I said, 'we only go for the big ones! We've just come back from the Miami Open.'

'Really? You're not very tanned ... '

'No,' said Rodney. 'Er, it was an indoor tournament.'

'Amazing, ain't it?' I said. 'They call it the Miami Open and then go and put walls round it. That's the yanks for you. Still, we can't complain. Hot Rod won it. Beat Jimmy Conelly in the final.'

'Don't you mean Jimmy Connors?'

'No,' I said. 'He knocked that didlo out in the first round, nine sets to one! We only nipped back to London so Hot Rod could get measured up for a new bat.'

'It's a raquet!' Nicky said.

'You're not wrong,' I said, 'the prices they charge!'

*F*ancy footwork

Pulling birds is all a question of footwork, and the Trotter boys were moving well. But sooner or later any reasonably bright bird is going to realise that some things don't add up. That's the moment to come clean.

'We're not really involved with professional tennis!' I confided.

They was gobsmacked. 'What do you really do?' they said as one.

'We're Concorde pilots ... '

Now there's just a chance they won't believe this, but never mind. You can all have a jolly good laugh and *voila*, in less than the time it takes to order a round of pina coladas you'll have their phone number on the back of your Castella packet.

And so it went that night. They had their own pad in Chelsea, and we agreed to pick them up the following Friday. As we aimed the E-Type towards Peckham, I knew we'd struck gold. It was the Klondike all over again.

As he lit me a celebratory Havana, Rodney could hardly control himself. The weekend at their place! He might even get to watch Match of the Day! And think of the money he'd save!

'Where's their number, Del?' he asked, mid-fantasy.

'On that cigar pack,' I said.

'Ace!' he said. Then there was a terrible pause. ''Er ... which cigar pack Del?'

'The one I just gave you.' I moved smoothly into fourth gear.

Rodney laughed nervously and glanced at the window. 'This is going to crease you right up ... '

'Go on then!' I said.

'I threw it out of the window about a mile and a half back ... '

I couldn't believe it! I stood on the anchors and the E-Type screeched to a halt. I was about to tell Rodney to search the entire length of the Old Kent Road on his hands and knees when I was rudely interrupted.

A Mark 2 Zephyr convertible with bald tyres, rust

spots and no brakes smashed into the back of us so hard it almost sent us into orbit.

When my head had cleared I realised I'd seen that motor somewhere before. I'd seen the driver and all. I paused only long enough to snatch the keys from the Jag's ignition before legging it in the direction of Camberwell Green.

If you follow the Trotter Way to Romance, the sight of an E-Type key ring will still get most birds as far as the car park. From then on, it depends whether they think they're being taken for a ride.

When it comes to romance, I've always been very much in the driving seat.

Different strokes for different blokes

If I had a quid for every time some bloke's come up to me in the Nag's Head and said: ''Ere, Del, you're a man of the world – what's the SP on putting a bit of sparkle back into my relationship?' I'd be a millionaire. I reckon there must be something about

the way I look that makes people come up to me and pour out their hearts. Most likely they see the aluminium briefcase, the keyring, the Filofax and the mobile phone and they think: blow me, it's Arnie Becker. He understands Roxanne's problems, I'll go and bend his ear hole a bit with mine.

Don't get me wrong, I don't mind doing it. I'll lend anyone a helping hand, but I'll be honest with you – I'd rather there was just a bit less lending and a bit more charging. I mean, them agony aunts make a bundle out of other people's problems, don't they? Anna RayBan, Irma Kurds, sorts like that. No way would you catch them or that Miriam Bollard leaning on the bar of the Nag's Head, dispensing their worldly wisdom free and gratis. No, they'd hold out for the

The Trotter Help-Lines are open.

price of a double Remy and lemonade at least, and that's what I reckon I should be doing.

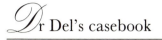r Del's casebook

Denzil came up to me one Monday with a bit of a marital problem. He'd managed to get a haulage contract the Friday before with this plastics factory over Deptford. The problem was, Friday was also his and Corinne's wedding anniversary, and he was faced with the classic romantic dilemma: what comes first – your money or your wife? Friday afternoon, see, he got an urgent call from the factory to go to a shop in High Wycombe and pick up fifty dolls. They were being returned, faulty stock. But he'd promised to take Corinne out for the evening, and by the time he got back through all the rush hour traffic it was half past six and he'd still got the dolls on board.

'So what was I supposed to do, Del?' he asked. 'Take them back to the factory like I'm supposed to and let Corinne down, or leave them on the truck until Monday and hope no one twigged?'

To a big, soppy romantic like me, the answer was blindingly obvious.

'You let Corinne down,' I said. After all, if a woman really loves you, she'll know how important it is for you to get a bit of business. Rodney, of course, thought different.

'How can the return of some faulty dolls be urgent?' he said. 'I'd have left them on my truck until Monday.'

'That's what I did,' said Denzil. 'And what happens? Saturday night the factory went up in flames. And tomorrow I've got to hand in this unsigned docket which proves I collected the dolls but also proves I didn't deliver them.'

For every negative there is a positive, that's what I say – in business, as in romance. I mean, it ain't the end of the world just because you find out you're on a blind date with a sort whose face looks like Picasso painted it. Just think of the price the Japs paid for his Sunflowers!

'This ain't a stroke of bad luck,' I declared. 'This is a gift from the gods!'

I took a pen from my pocket and signed it with Friday's date. They'd be too busy to check it, and as far as they were concerned the dolls would have gone up in flames with the rest of the factory. Then I gave Denzil a hundred quid for them. The owners would get more insurance money, Denzil got an empty van and a hundred nicker bunce, me and Rodders got fifty dollies to flog down the market and the great British public got another bargain of a lifetime! *Petit dejeuner!* Sometimes I surprise even myself with the power of my vision.

Unfortunately, it wasn't till we got the dollies home that I found out they weren't quite the top of the range Sindies or Barbies I'd been counting on. No, these dollies had slightly more foreign sounding names.

'This one's called Erotic Estelle,' Rodney read on the first box. 'Oh and look, here's Lusty Linda.'

'They're big for little dolls, ain't they?' Albert asked. If his powers of observation were as good as that when he was up in the crow's nest, it's not surprising he spent half his naval career treading water.

'No, no, Unc,' said Rodney. 'They're not ordinary dolls, they're the sort you see being advertised in magazines – you know, seedy magazines, for tacky, sleazy little men.'

'You're pulling my leg,' said Uncle Albert, who obviously ain't been round

72   the world quite as many

*R*odney had what psychiatrists call a 'thing' about uniforms.

times as he claims to have been.

'Oh, am I?' said Rodney, producing a copy of *Uniforms Monthly* from his inside pocket as evidence.

While Albert cast a connoisseur's eye over the centrefold, I did some quick thinking. Imagine a big romantic like me being caught with an inflatable doll in the flat – let alone fifty. I mean, I've done a bit of two-timing in my love life, but never with half a regiment.

'We'll have to get rid of them a bit lively,' I announced, chucking them both out of sight behind the fridge.

'Cor, look at the prices they sell for,' said Albert. 'Sixty pounds each.'

'On the other hand,' I said, 'let's not be too hasty.'

The inflated cost of loving

Think of the love, romance and companionship these harmless objects could bring to lonely old men. I reckoned Trig would have two or three of them, straight off.

I looked at one of the leaflets. The dolls in Rodney's magazine fetched sixty quid a piece but they were well downmarket compared with ours. Nowhere near as good looking, neither. No question about it, we'd struck gold. Our dolls were the real business – self-inflating de luxe models, for the more discerning weirdo. If we could sell them at thirty nicker each we'd make fourteen hundred quid profit!

I knew who'd buy them off us, and all – Dirty Barry, owner of a little personal shop I know just off the Walworth Road. Many's the client of mine who's got straight in a cab after a consultation at the Nag's and headed down to Dirty Barry's to buy himself a few bits and pieces for a therapy session. It always makes me happy to think I've made a fellow human being happy. My ten per cent commission is just the icing on the cake.

'I don't want to have nothing to do with them, Del!' Rodney said again.

To me, it was simple. We're supposed to be traders,

and that's all we would be doing – trading. It was just a one off deal. I mean, some people make their living out of this sort of thing, and it's big business and all. You read in the Sunday papers about these MPs and even vicars who go to Soho vice dens and get whipped and beaten up, and pay two hundred quid for the privilege. They should take a walk round this estate one night, they'd get it done free on the National Health!

No, I know these sort of people are sick, but they're still human beings. And if some pervo wants to get it going with half a pound of laytex and a lump of oxygen that's his business. As far as I'm concerned, the romantic in me says he can have a meaningful relationship with a barrage balloon – as long as it's in the privacy of its own hangar. And if I can help by flogging them nirvana at thirty quid a throw, well, that's both of us happy. Everyone's a winner!

There was an uneasy silence while Rodney and Albert digested my thoughts, but it was soon broken by a sound like air escaping from a narrow gap in the valve of a balloon. Rodney and I immediately looked at Albert.

'What are you looking at me for?' he asked, the picture of offended innocence.

'Well, most funny sounds in this flat tend to emanate from your vicinity,' Rodney said.

Romance for the more discerning weirdo

The sound came again, only this time it was in short, sharp bursts. We went into the kitchen, following the hissing noise that was now followed by the sound of a large air bubble rushing to the surface.

Suddenly a ghostly white doll popped up from behind the fridge.

'I've seen this happen before!' exclaimed the old man of the sea. 'Years ago I was in Jamaica and I saw a voodoo ceremony. This witch-doctor ran his hands over a dead cat and it came back to life.'

There was a bubbling and hissing sound again and now a dusky-coloured inflatable popped up.

75

'That's you talking about Jamaica!' I said. 'I don't understand it. I thought you'd have to pull a cord or press a button to inflate them.'

They were jammed up against the hot air duct; there must have been little canisters of gas inside them that were triggered off by the heat. Whatever, we had to do something quickly, before the rest of the Black and White Minstrels popped up.

'They're bound to have a valve on them,' I said. 'Go on then, Rodney, have a look for it.'

'I'm not looking for it,' Rodney said. It could be . . . anywhere!'

'I ain't looking for it either,' said Albert. 'Could be illegal.'

'Well, they ain't going to call for the police, are they!' I said.

Cor blimey, do it yourself Del.

I found the valve and started pushing a matchstick into it. Rodney did the same with his doll.

'Did Monica let you do this?' I asked.

I find that with Rodney it's important to keep open the channels of communication regarding his relationships. I want him to feel that he can come to me at any time and talk anything through.

'Shut up, Del.'

Well, that's the thanks you get for caring.

I kept pushing with my matchstick but nothing happened.

'Maybe they're dodgy valves,' Albert said. 'We used to get them on the rubber dinghies in the navy. Once they're up they won't come down.'

'So how are you going to explain away the fact to Dirty Barry that they're fully inflated?' Rodney asked.

'I'll tell him they're samples,' I said. 'I'll say we blew them up so that he could see them in all their beauty.'

Go out with a bang

Well, as I've said to more birds than I can remember, not every love story can have a happy ending. Uncle
Albert and me turned up at the tradesmen's entrance

of Ecstasy (Suppliers of Adult Requisites) to find the place locked and bolted. I banged on the door and there was a great crashing of chains.

'He's security conscious, ain't he?' Albert said.

'That's not security,' I said, 'he's moving some of his stock!'

A few boxes of chains, whips and studded leathers collars later, the door slid to one side and there was Dirty Barry in all his sleazy glory.

'Buying or selling?' he asked.

'Selling,' I said.

'Yeah? What?'

'What do you mean, 'What?'!' I said. 'These things of course! What did you think I was doing with them, giving them a guided tour?'

Barry didn't want to know. Apparently the bottom had fallen out of the market, thanks to the government and their moral crusade. Dirty Barry'd had a visit from the council and they'd revoked his licence. Closed him down. He'd flogged off his entire stock, four hundred dolls, that very morning – for fifteen quid each.

Just my luck. If I'd bought the things a couple of days ago I could have outed them by now. Instead of which Dirty Barry and his mates had flooded the market. So he'd got rid of his stock but there was me lumbered with Polythene Pam and Vinyl Vera. Still, I have a theory. Business is a bit like romance – one minute you're up, the next you're down. I'd just hang on to them and wait for the next Big Bang.

Unfortunately the next big bang was a lot closer than any of us realised. 'You'd better not be having me on, Rodney,' I said after he'd told me what had been on the news. 'I'll whack you straight in the mouth if you're pulling my leg.'

We were running out of the flat at the time, Rodney spraying cold water over the dolls with a plant spray to keep them cool.

Apparently it wasn't oxygen they'd got the dolls going with, but propane. Due to a technical error, they had been loaded with highly explosive and volatile gases. The old bill said they were potentially lethal, particularly when exposed to heat, and were appealing for their immediate return. If Erotic Estelle and her mates had got hot they'd have had to re-do the A to Z!

We jumped into the three-wheeler and I drove at breakneck speed to the wasteland on Herrington Road. Then we grabbed the dolls out of the back and chucked them down an embankment. With a mixture of relief at our escape and sorrow at the loss of sixty quids' worth of stock, I looked over the edge and saw that they'd landed next to a couple of old winos who were sitting by a fire.

'It's all right,' I shouted down, 'just dropping them off.'

The winos looked dead impressed. They were obviously fellow members of the masterful school of romance.

It was as we were walking back to the van that the explosion occurred . . .

Looking down the edge of the embankment again, I saw the winos' faces looking up – a bit astonished, mud and brickdust landing all around them.

I shrugged my shoulders.

'I told them not to have that mutton vindaloo!' I said.

The moral of this story is that it don't matter what kind of bird you get mixed up with – one wrong move and the results can be very explosive. And another moral is: if you happen to know a discerning weirdo who's in the market for forty-eight inflatable dolls, you've got my address.

You Always Remember the First Time

When it comes to romance, I reckon there ain't been a single great lover in history, from Don Juan to Don Johnson, who don't remember his first doink. I mean, it's like the death of Kennedy, your first bit of humpty dumpty – you always remember exactly where you were and, if you're a soppy old romantic like me, who you were with.

One poor bloke with no romantic memories, good or bad, is Trig, but that don't stop him trying. He came into the Nag's a little while back wearing all his best gear – the brown two piece suit, the purple shirt, and the orange tie, all topped off nicely with the technicolour V-neck. When I saw him I thought either it must be Comic Relief day again or he was following the David Ike Way to Romance. Then I clocked the small spray of flowers in his hand and I knew at once what was up.

Trig was on a *date!*

It's hard to know the right advice about romance to offer someone like Trig, specially when the Trotters are in the Nag's in force. See, there are actually three Trotter Ways to Romance – there's Albert's way, there's Rodney's Way, and then there's the Way That Works.

Uncle Albert's idea of the perfect woman was always a dancing girl from a Cairo nightclub with a silver G-string and a ruby in her belly-button. To him, foreplay was a glass of date liqueur and a ten dinar note.

Rodney is a totally different kettle of fish. Two halves of lager in the British Legion club is like a walk on the wild side to him.

As for me, well, I'm here to tell you there's no place for small thinkers in the modern world, in business or in romance. As I keep telling Rodney, in both you've got to be big, brave and brazen. Anyway, I took my hat off to Trig. In fact, I even ordered him a large scotch.

'How did you know I wanted a scotch?' he asked.

''Cos if I was dressed like that I'd want a scotch!' I said.

'So who's the lucky lady?' I asked Trig. 'Anyone we know?'

'You don't know her,' he said. 'Come to that I don't know her either.'

Turned out Trig had been to a computerised dating firm to get himself fixed up. 'Course, I've never needed one of them places (and nor will you if you follow The Trotter Way To Romance) so I had to get Trig to explain a bit about it.

'They've just opened up down the High Street,' he said. 'I thought I'd have twenty-five quids' worth, see what occurs. They fed all my information into a computer and it came out with a woman who was compatible with me.'

Even now I go weak at the knees when I try to imagine what a woman who's compatible with Trig would look like.

'What I like about this agency,' Trig went on, 'is you know where you stand with them – they insist on honesty.'

'So you told them you're a roadsweeper?' I said.

'No, I said I was a bus inspector, to add a bit of glamour.'

I didn't think much more of it, to be honest, until I was out in the car park a bit later. Then I saw Trig and his date arriving at the Italian place opposite ...

and if I tell you she was in her mid-thirties, slim, smartly-dressed and had a great pair of lungs on her, you'll understand why I decided right there and then that if I was to carry on giving Trig the benefit of my romantic wisdom, I owed it to him to go and visit the Technomatch Friendship and Matrimonial Agency myself, in person.

*T*aking down your particulars

'So tell me,' said the bloke behind the computer, 'what kind of person are you looking for?'

'Well ... ' I said, ' ... a bird.'

'But are there particular requirements?' he asked.

Yes, of course there were, and you'd do well to make a note of them for your own benefit, 'cos this is just another area where if you don't follow Del Trotter's advice you could find yourself waiting until Millwall win the UEFA Cup before you get your card stamped. So:

1. She must be a local bird if possible – you don't want to spend too much on petrol.
2. She must be refined. You don't want a night out with some old bow wow who don't know the difference between a Liebfraumilk and a can of Tizer.
3. Be completely honest. There is very little future in fabrication or deceit.

'I'm sorry, I've forgotten,' the bloke said as he took my twenty-five quid. 'Is there an E on the end of your name?'

'No E,' I said. 'It's Duval. Derek Duval. It's from the French side of my family.'

I got to Waterloo station bang on time next day with a big bunch of flowers. According to the bloke at the agency it's rather traditional, and in its way quite romantic. Apparently it also evokes memories of some bloke called Trevor and a Celia sort, but he wouldn't give me the SP on how they did in the humpty stakes.

I was meeting a bird called Raquel – Raquel Turner, the actress. She did Chekov mostly, West End. You might have heard of her. Anyway, I hoped she was on her toes – the last bird I'd met at Waterloo station had got mugged on the escalator.

*L*egal, decent, honest and truthful

*R*omance is often a matter of being in the right place at the right time.

'This is a bit like Brief Encounter, isn't it?' Raquel said as we walked towards a cab. 'That's my favourite film.'

A little bit of mistletoe knocks them bandy.

'Mine as well,' I said. 'I loved the bit at the end when the big space ship landed and all them little martians came out.'

The restaurant was a blinder. I got us all set up with the wine and starters and what have you, then nipped out to have a quick word with the head waiter. He didn't seem used to the ways of big business, but a twenty quid note soon sorted that out.

'Sorry about that,' I said to Raquel. 'I just had to get a message to an old friend.'

'Oh that's okay. This is wonderful.' Raquel sipped her wine nervously.

I understood: she probably felt a bit out of her depth in my ostentatious company.

She told me she'd been married before but it was a disaster. 'And I've had – you know – relationships with men which have always ended unhappily,' she said. 'Maybe it's been the same for you?'

'No,' I said, 'blokes don't do a lot for me.'

We got on like a house on fire, Raquel and me. She told me all about herself, openly and honestly, and I did the same, especially about being the managing director of one of Britain's biggest import/export businesses, with several residences worldwide and a red Ferrari.

'I gave up acting for nine years while I was married,' she said. 'My husband was one of those old-fashioned types who thought there should be only one bread winner.'

'Yeah, my Dad was like that,' I said. 'He used to get up at six every morning to get my Mum off to work.'

The head waiter came to our table.

'Mr Duval.'

'Yes?'

'I'm terribly sorry to bother you, sir, but there's an important call from your New York office.'

I excused myself and stood up. Then I changed my mind and sat down again.

'Charles,' I said, 'tell them I'm busy.'

I smiled at Raquel.

'I'm enjoying your company and I'm not going to

have it spoilt by some soppy problem in New York. Them yanks have got to learn to make decisions for themselves.'

When to use the handcuffs

Nigh on a hundred and fifty quid that date with Raquel cost me, but it wasn't until I'd forked out another fifty that I saw her with her clothes off. It wasn't exactly how I'd have planned it, though, and here's another important lesson to be learnt.

It was Albert's birthday that week and I'd organised a party for him at the Nag's. Raquel couldn't come because she was off rehearsing a play somewhere. It was a pity, that, because I wanted her to meet the family. Anyway, the party was going well. I could tell because Albert had started slurring his words at the bar.

'He's almost offended some of the ladies,' Mike complained. 'He wanted a rum and black but he ordered a bum and rack!'

'Well keep your fingers crossed he don't fancy a Bucks Fizz, Michael!' I said.

It was just then that a naval officer in full uniform marched into the bar, accompanied by a Wren. They both looked dead officious as they strode up to the piano.

'Able Seaman Albert Trotter, late of His Majesty's ship Peerless?' the officer demanded.

'Aye, aye, sir,' the old sea dog replied.

'I'm placing you under arrest. You will be taken to the naval stockade, Portsmouth, where you will await court martial. Read the charges, Petty Officer.'

'Aye aye, sir,' the Wren barked as she produced some paperwork and began to read. 'Able Seaman Albert Trotter. You are hereby ordered by Her Majesty the Queen, the High Lords of the Admiralty and by all your friends and relatives to have a very happy birthday!'

What a blinder! But the best was yet to come ... the Wren tore off her shirt and tie to reveal a skimpy black bra. Then she sat on Albert's lap and started singing Slow Boat To China.

'Is this your birthday surprise?' asked Rodney.

'Yeah,' I said, wiping the tears from my eyes. 'I saw this strippergram firm in the local paper. I've done him up like a kipper, Rodney. Look at the old sod's face.'

But all eyes were on the Wren. Still on Albert's knee, she was now pulling off her skirt to reveal stockings and a suspender belt and ...

It was when she swivelled in his lap and turned to face the audience that I realised who it was.

'Raquel?' I choked.

She looked at me and just shook her head slowly.

'Raquel?' Boycie guffawed. 'Is this the actress you've been telling us about?'

He roared with laughter. So did everybody else. I was hurt, deeply hurt. I was filled with rage and embarrassment – but above all, disappointment. I just stared at her. I wanted to cry, I wanted to die, but instead I just turned and walked out of the pub, laughter and derision echoing in my ears. So much for bloody romance, eh? And what about my two hundred quid?

I stormed out into the car park and went up to the van. I stopped a moment and looked up at the heavens. I wanted to punch, I wanted to kill, I wanted to burst into tears and melt into the tarmac. I thumped the roof and kicked the tyre, then fell against the van, exhausted with anger and frustration.

'Alright?' beamed Rodney, who'd followed me out.

'Oddly enough, Rodney,' I said, 'I am not alright.'

Raquel rushed out of the pub, covered by the officer's topcoat. 'Look, this is probably a daft question,' she said, 'but do you want to see any more of me?'

I didn't think there was much more to see.

'Yeah, I'd like to see you again, sweetheart,' I said. 'But next time I'll pay at the door like the other punters.'

And there's your lesson. If you tell a bird you want her to meet your family, just make sure she's got her bloody clothes on when she does.

*D*on't take it lying down

I was a little out of sorts after the strippergram episode, I can tell you. Well, it's not every day the love of your life flashes her thruppenny bits at your mates, is it – and if it is, you're probably not the kind of person who needs this book.

I was sitting in Sid's cafe a few days later, reading my paper, when Rodney said something that made me look up.

'Raquel, what a lovely surprise!' he said. 'Look who's here, Del. Have you got time for a cup of tea, Raquel?'

'I don't know,' she replied, looking at me with doleful eyes. 'Have I got time for a cup of tea?'

'It's a free country, I said.

'There you are,' Rodney smiled at Raquel as he got up and left us together. 'I told you he'd mellow after a while.'

'I've resigned from the strippergram agency,' she said. 'I've signed on the dole.'

'It's a step up the ladder, ain't it?' I said.

Raquel looked at me for a second or two then dropped a right old bombshell. She was going on tour in the Middle East – a revue, dancing, that sort of thing. Blimey, you read about that sort of thing in the Sunday papers. She'd end up as an hostess in some topless dive in the kasbah!

Any Time . . . Any Place . . . Anywhere
. . . The Trotter Way to Romance . . . The Right One.

I've always been very well hung.

'It's a shame the two of us couldn't have been more honest with each other,' she said.

'I was straight with you ... ' I said. 'All right, I said my name was Duval. That's nothing, is it? Just a joke!'

Sid beckoned for me to go up to the counter.

'What's he want?' I asked.

'Maybe it's another call from your New York office,' she said.

I smiled.

She smiled back.

I went up to Sid and collected my breakfast.

'Del, I just want to say thanks,' Raquel said when I got back.

'What for?'

90

'For a lot of things. For being the only man I've

ever met who wanted me to keep my clothes on. For – I don't know – giving me back some self-esteem ... I used to wake up in the morning and look in the mirror and think, Oh you again! But after I met you I used to wake up and think, Great, another day, you're going to be somebody! This time next year I'll be famous. Thanks for that.'

Even Douglas Fairbanks would have been moved by that one. I'm man enough to admit that I was. I looked into her eyes.

'Raquel –' I found it hard to find the words. The right ones never come when you need them. 'Would you like a bit of my fried bread?'

Saying bonjour

We chatted on, more and more easily. But it all boiled down to the fact that she was leaving the next day. She had a cab coming at twelve to take her to Waterloo station. Byronic, wasn't it?

'It doesn't have to be the end, Del,' she said. 'We could still go on seeing each other.'

'Yeah, I'll pop over to Addis Ababa and catch the show,' I said.

'I meant I don't have to go ... ' she said.

This was dangerous ground. I mean, a bit of romance is all very well, but you can get too much of a good thing. I didn't know what to say.

'I've done all my thinking, Del, and I know what I want. If you want me to stay then I will. And I'm not talking about any heavy commitment like marriage or even living together. We could just – be there for each other. Think about it, won't you?'

'Yeah, of course I will.'

'If you like the idea then just be at my flat tomorrow,' Raquel said as she got up to leave. 'If not, I'll understand.'

Can a tiger change his spots?

I've always been bad luck to women. I've always left them with nothing but aggro ... I'm a bit like that 91

Little Joe in Bonanza. Not in looks – he's an ugly git. What I mean is, if you watch an episode of Bonanza and Little Joe falls in love with a woman, you know she's going to die. The moment he starts stronging it with a sort you can guarantee she's going to catch a fever, get trampled in a stampede or the Indians are going to have her.

But that wouldn't happen to Raquel, I decided. She had come after me. She'd had to swallow her pride, that took a lot of doing. In my book that made her a bit special. So I said to myself: whatever happens Raquel will not end up full of arrows.

In fact, I was just having a sharpener down the Nag's before going round to her flat when in came a pair of old bill. They came straight over to where I was sitting.

'Is your name Trotter?' the young constable asked.

'That's me,' I smiled.

'Is that your yellow van out there?' said the very pretty WPC.

'What, the one with Trotter written on it?' I asked. 'Yes, that's mine.'

'A couple of weeks ago a yellow three-wheeled van, very similar to yours, shot the lights of Lewisham Hill and Woodford Lane,' the constable said. 'We're in the process of questioning the owners of all such vehicles.'

'Look no further, officer,' I said, going over to Albert at the piano. 'It was me! It's a fair cop, I done it!'

I shook my head at Albert. I knew he said he'd get his own back on me for the naval officer stunt, but I really expected something a bit more original than this.

'You've disappointed me, Uncle,' I said, turning to face the WPC. 'Look, I'm a bit pushed for time, darling,' I said, 'so can we get a move on? Come on then, show us what you've got.'

'What do you mean?' she demanded.

There was no time for argument. Raquel would be getting into that cab soon, so it was time for a bit of he who dares wins. I took hold of the buttons on her tunic and ripped it open. Lovely sight it was, too, even if the bra were a bit more sensible looking than the black lacy peek-a-boo number Raquel had been wearing the night of her big turn. I was just about to tell Albert I appreciated the joke when I happened to look out of the window.

Parked outside was a Metro – one of them white ones, with red stripes along the side and a blue light on the top.

'Sorry,' I grinned, as I tried to help the girl do up her buttons. 'Not half as sorry as you're going to be, cocker,' she snapped.

And that was that, really. I even tried bribery, but

*W*hen it comes to romance, I've always thought two thirds of the Trotter family should be kept behind bars.

they ended up doing me with that and all. Ten minutes later I was down at the police station, being charged.

'Can I at least use the phone?' I asked the desk sergeant.

'You're allowed one phone call,' he said.

'Thank you. What's the time?' he asked.

'Twenty to one.'

'Triffic!' I said. 'You don't know the code for Addis Ababa do you?'

The real thing

Any big player in the romance game has to recognise the difference between a bit of slap'n'tickle in the back of the van and The Real Thing. The trouble is, falling in love ain't as easy as it looks. I've been engaged more times than a switchboard, so I should know. But it's always special, and it usually happens when you're least expecting it – at the fishmongers; over a Pina Collada at The Purple Pussycat; even at night school – as Rodney found out:

Thursday

I am in love. Her name is Cassandra and I met her at yesterday's evening class. Now, twenty-four hours later, the smell of her perfume still assaults my senses. It's probably because I'm wearing her trenchcoat in bed as I write this.

I recall the events of last night so clearly, and you can't say that about a lot of nights. Sure, it began ordinarily enough, with me running a programme through the Rhaja computer amongst the sauce bottles on what Del calls his boardroom table.

'That's the way Rodney,' Uncle Albert says, coming in from the kitchen. 'Don't bother helping me get the tea ready; you carry on poncing about with that computer.'

My fingers stop dancing, momentarily, across the keyboard.

'I am not "poncing about" with anything!' I say witheringly. 'In case it has slipped that senile, shrapnel-cluttered brain of yours, I am studying for a diploma in computer science!'

How I wished, at that moment, for someone to understand. Someone who would instinctively grasp my dreams and aspirations and instead of drowning them in a bucket, let them fly. Someone sensitive, who wouldn't be fooled by my tough, macho exterior, but would recognise the poetry in my soul. Now I know that that someone is Cassandra.

We met after the class. I'm looking through my homework and thinking bloody hell, how am I supposed to get through this? Suddenly I am aware of her presence. Her voice sings to me.

'I'm sorry to interrupt you,' she says.

'Oh, it's nothing,' I say. 'Just some computer data that I have to set in a programme.' I can see she's impressed. I get slowly to my feet. 'My name's Rodney,' I say.

'Cassandra,' comes her reply.

Our hands mingle. I'm playing it very cool.

'I'm glad we bumped into each other,' I say. 'I was trying to figure out a way of saying hello. I think it's really kind of liberated for you to make the first move.'

'Move?' she says. 'No, you don't understand! You've taken my coat!'

I have! And I feel a right zonk!! But I can't help noticing she's taken mine too. I offer to walk her to her car. Unfortunately it's parked right outside the building. It only takes about twenty seconds.

'Thank you for getting me here safely,' she says.

I flex my shoulders and put on my macho voice, which is probably a mistake. 'Think nothing of it!' I want it to sound like the bloke who does the Denim ads, but it comes out more like a Rottweiler ordering lunch.

She smiles again. I can't believe it! She's beautiful. She's in her dad's BMW, and she's offering me a lift to the bus station! I'm about to get in when I hear a voice in the distance calling my name. Shit! I pretend not to hear it.

'Rodders, over here! Come on, I'll give you a lift home!'

The game's up. Everyone in the bloody street heard Del that time. I'll say one thing for my brother, he's an absolute

especially when it comes to my love life.

I was touched when I first read this, very touched. He don't often show his appreciation of all I've done for him, but there it is, in black and white. Del Trotter, an absolute diamond. I still blush to think of it.

'Who's the tart?' I asked, as I led him into this wine bar I'd discovered across the street. I told Rodders I'd been in there since I'd dropped him off. Chatted up a couple of yuppy sorts, told them a few jokes, flashed the Filofax, knocked them bandy.

'So where are they now?' he asked.

I looked around and shrugged. 'Don't know,' I said. 'They went to the ladies a couple of hours ago and ain't come back since! Still, never mind, plenty more where they come from. While we're here, why don't we pull a couple more and go on to a club?'

He wasn't as cheerful about this as I'd expected. 'Not me Del,' he said. 'I'm off.'

'Excuse me,' the barman said as I watched Rodders leave, 'are you eating?'

'Not me, John,' I said, twanging my Gordon Gecko braces. 'Dinner is for wimps.'

On the money

Rodders went around for days looking like he'd had a promise from a liar. Then suddenly, one night, his long hours studying the Trotter Way to Romance paid off. And believe me, if he can do it, so can you.

He'd gone off to a disco with Mickey Pearce and Jevon, Peckham's answer to Eddie Murphy. I wish I'd been there.

Sunday

Last night was cosmic! Even walking home in the rain after Cassie had dropped me outside one of those big houses in King's Avenue didn't spoil it. She kissed me! My only worry is that sooner or later I'll have to admit I don't live there.

Mickey and Jevon are gobsmacked. I'm sitting at the bar for hours listening to them talk about their conquests, then I walk away with tonight's star prize!

I can still hear them. Mickey's eyes are darting around the dance floor. 'See that blonde bird?' he says. 'I've had her! See that black sort at the back there? Crazy about me. Phones me all the time!'

'You're a hell of a man, Mickey,' Jevon says.

I raise my eyes from my lager and ask him if he's doing it for charity.

'What do you mean!' he says.

'I wondered if it was a sponsored bullshit?'

Two birds pass by and wave at Jevon.

'Not dancing tonight?' they ask.

'Not at this precise moment in time,' he says. 'But, being a creature of impulse, I am coiled like a spring, ready to move with sinuous grace when the music takes me. If either of you two should be in the vicinity when this occurs, then who knows, it could be your lucky night!'

He turns back to us, beaming. I don't know how he does it. Snapping his fingers he says: 'Ok - I've given you two losers an audience, and now it's time for me to do what I was put on this earth to do - bring pleasure and excitement into the lives of attractive young women. And this evening's lucky winner is the chick at the corner table.

I haven't seen her, but Mickey's been monitoring developments closely. 'You've got no chance, Jevon. Five blokes have asked her to dance already, and she gave them all a blank.'

'Five ordinary mortals,' says Jevon, standing. 'She hasn't met me yet.'

'You go ahead, Jevon,' I say. 'We'll prepare the altar.'

'I'll wave to you as we leave,' he says.

'That Jevon really does the business, don't he Rodney?' Mickey says. 'Not surprising, though. I taught him all he knows.'

'Turn it up Mickey,' I say. 'The last time you went out with a bird you took her to a Bay City Rollers concert!'

'I don't believe it!' he says, looking over my shoulder. 'Jevon's fallen on stony ground!'

I turn. Jevon's fighting to stay in the game, but he's losing. I blink. I don't believe it! The bird who's giving him the thumbs down is Cassandra! She waves and says 'Hi!' To me!

'She's a lesbian,' Jevon explains when he gets back to the bar.

'Quick Rodney, phone the AA. Tell them the sex machine's broken down!' Mickey says, swinging into action. 'It's time for you to watch the Master and learn.'

He's back with us almost before he's gone.

'Well?' we ask.

He doesn't look happy. 'Definitely a lesbian!'

'She'll dance with me,' I say, keeping everything crossed.

For some reason this cracks them up.

'Look,' Mickey says, 'I'm a first Dan of lateral chatting, and Jevon is God's foster son. So what chance has a wally like you got?'

I'm not fazed. 'I bet she will!'

Two tenners hit the bar before you could shake a stick at them.

A minute later I'm on the dance floor, twenty quid richer and Cassandra in my arms. I'm in love.

*E*ven Micky Pearce and Jevon have suffered the odd emotional scar.

I'll never forget how he looked when he got back. Soaked to the skin with a dead soppy grin on his face. Mickey Pearce had said he'd been given a lift home by some posh tart, but he hadn't told me she was driving a convertible. I thought they must have taken a short cut through a car wash.

*M*eeting the relatives

I knew it wouldn't be long before I was called upon to give Cassie the once over. I'll admit there have been times when I've misjudged the appeal of the odd consignment of merchandise, but as Rodney well knew, I'm spot on with women.

I chose the One Eleven Club as a good place to meet. It's Peckham's answer to Monty Carlo. Dead classy, done out in early Barbara Cartland, and there was more flesh on display than on Sainsbury's poultry counter. I was just doing a deal on some gold chains when they arrived. One glance told me she was a bit of alright.

'Rodney's told me *all* about you,' I smiled. 'But don't worry, I'm not the type to shout it about.'

'That's nice of you Derek,' she said. 'Rodney's told me all about you as well, although I didn't believe him – until now!'

In the bedroom, as in the boardroom, I've always enjoyed the cut and thrust and to and fro of open, honest, well-honed verbal exchange. 'Course, it sometimes gets out of hand and you end up having to clump somebody, but that's all part of the fun.

'I like her,' I said to Rodney, sensing that she really was special to him. 'Have you given her one?'

Me and Cassie hit it off from the start, and the most amazing thing was her old man grew up on a nearby council estate, BMW or no BMW.

'What's his name?' I said. 'Maybe I know him.'

'Oh God,' said Rodney, for reasons best known to him.

'Parry,' Cassy said. 'Alan Parry.'

'Know him well!' I said. 'Little fellow, one blue eye, one brown, talks with a squint, walks with a stutter?'

'That's him!' she said, and we both laughed.

I knew this was the big one for Rodney when I saw them both later in her dad's car. He wasn't letting her 99 come up for air. At one point she had her whole head in his mouth. The last time I saw anything like that was in a circus.

*S*helling out for the wedding

Let's face it, marriage ain't everybody's cup of tea. On the other hand, it's very popular with the punters. I know quite a few who liked it so much they even did it twice. Elizabeth Taylor's on eight and counting. But that don't change the fact that it's a bit of a turn-up when it happens to someone in your own family.

All these thoughts and more were running through my mind when I bumped into Alan, Cassandra's dad, just after Rodney had got himself engaged. We'd got together once already and we'd got on like a house on fire. He'd been so legless at the end of the evening that I even managed to flog him a mobile phone. It had given him a nasty bruise where the aerial had hit him in the eye.

'Hello you old toerag,' he greeted me. He may have a few grand on the hip, Alan, but success ain't spoiled him. 'I thought I'd pop down and see you about the wedding arrangements. I think it's right that you should make a contribution to the proceedings.'

I suddenly went very still. 'Yeah,' I said. 'Of course...'

'I mean, what sort of hall do you think we should hire?'

Funny, they don't go into things like this in the Martini ads. Let this be a warning to you. Romance ain't all crushed ice and Ferraris. Having said that, I only ever wanted the best for my bruv.

'Well,' I said, 'they're only having a registry office wedding, so we don't have to go mad. Mike's got a nice hall above here, you know. And it'll be cheap.'

Alan nodded. 'If I had my way that's exactly where we'd hold the reception. A good old knees-up in a pub and plenty of jellied eels.'

'Well this place is perfect then, ain't it?' I said.

'Yeah,' Alan said, 'but my wife Pam has gone up market. She wants to hold the reception at the cricket pavilion or a country club. She's got it all worked out, complete with Dom Perignon and caviar.'

I didn't know what to say.

'Not a jellied eel in sight! So what do you think?'

'I think you should put your foot down.' I swallowed hard. 'How much is this going to cost me?'

'Cost you?' Alan said. 'It won't cost you a penny, Del. My only child is getting married and I'm paying for the lot!'

'You said you wanted me to make a contribution . . .'

'Yeah,' he said, 'with ideas and opinions.'

'Oh!' I said. 'Well you know, your Mrs has got a point, ain't she? I mean, you and me mustn't be selfish. We've got to think of the happy couple. It's their big day!'

'But you don't like those kind of surroundings, do you Del? Champagne, caviar and country clubs!'

*H*appy Families.

'Hate it, Alan, hate it!' I said, raising my Remy and cream soda once more to my lips. 'I mean, it's all put on, ain't it? Them sort of people just do things for effect!'

May the best man win

I've always thought of myself as a caviar person, probably, but you know, when it came to it, it was a cracker of a do. I was a bit cut up at the time, partly because, well, I was sad to see Rodney go, and partly because the Driscoll brothers had given me a right good hammering on account of some mobile phones they hadn't been paid for.

There were some difficult moments on the big day, but which father of the bride hasn't overdone the

*R*odney Charlton Trotter's Big Day.

jellied eels at the reception and chucked the lot up in the khazi? It's all part of the fun. And which groom hasn't dreaded the moment when the registrar looks you straight in the eye and lets all your mates know your middle name?

'Do you, Rodney Charlton Trotter . . . '

I tell you, Mickey Pearce and Jevon laughed so hard they was almost handed the red card.

So there we were. Or rather, there I was. Rodders had a new wife, a new job, a new flat, a new life. And judging by the fact that he went through his entire honeymoon without catching a sun tan, that's not all he was having.

It wasn't all plain sailing, though. He came back to Nelson Mandela House after his first day at Alan's printing firm looking terrible. His three piece suit, smart tie and trendy raincoat were in great shape, but he was cream crackered.

'What is it?' I asked, as he flopped down in his usual armchair. 'Executive stress?'

'No, it's that bike,' he said. 'The wheels hardly turn, the chain's come off twice and the front light don't work. Where did you get it from?'

'God knows bruv,' I said. 'It's been in the garage for years.'

'What's for tea?' he said, yawning.

It was time to take him in hand again.

'Can I just say something to you?' I said. 'Give you a piece of advice that might stand you in good stead for the future?'

He nodded, but he wasn't really there. 'Yeah, go on then.'

'You see Rodney, how can I put it? *You don't live here any more!*'

There was silence for a moment, then a blood-curdling yell.

'Bloody hell, she'll go loopy!'

He took off down the stairs like he'd got a person to person call from God. As I watched him go, I realised with a smile that no matter how things might seem, romance don't change everybody. Rodders was still a forty-two carrot plonker.

Keeping it Together

Getting it together ain't easy, but keeping it together's a git. I don't know why, but Rodders and Cassie had difficulties from the start. It may have had something to do with Rodney punching her boss at a dinner party – I know she takes her job at the bank very seriously. Still, as Raquel says, a lot of people think that marriage comes complete with gift-wrapping, but it don't. It comes in kit form. You've got to work at it.

Judging by his diary, this wasn't a concept

It's all about images.

Rodney had taken on board. What follows is the
Rodney Trotter step-by-step guide to an early divorce:

Wednesday

That does it! I'm leaving.

I get back last night after a terrible journey round the one way system to discover Cassandra - my wife - on her way out. She ain't even cooked me my dinner!

'What's it tonight?' I say with heavy irony. 'The _bank's_ final exams? The _bank's_ annual cheese and wine orgy? The _bank's_ yoga and target practice course?'

'I'm playing badminton,' she says.

'Oh, I see,' I say. 'Where?'

'The bank's sports club.'

'Great,' I say. 'You go and enjoy yourself Cassandra. I've got a busy evening ahead as well. I'm going to sit in and read the _bank's_ pamphlet on our joint pension policy!'

'If you don't stop being so childish,' she says, 'I swear one of these days I'll smother you with your comfort blanket!'

Childish, me?! She's the one who's got to start growing up. When's she going to realise she's got a marriage, a home, a husband, me?

'I never see you,' I say. 'You use this flat like base camp! I've had double glazing salesmen spend more time in here than you! You're always out - on your own!'

'I've asked you to badminton a million times,' she says, 'but you always refuse!'

I sigh deeply. 'Because I don't relish the idea of spending an entire evening whacking a dead budgie over a net! Besides, all our social occasions are in some way tied to the _bank!_'

She goes very still. 'You resent me pursuing a career, don't you?'

I disagree vigorously. I admire anyone who tries to advance themselves, but her ideas of advancement come straight out of Rommel's A Thousand and One Things Every Good Panzer General Should Know! It's relentless! It's Blitzkrieg! And she claims it's just her trying to make up lost ground after I clumped her boss in the face!

She keeps bloody mentioning that, and I didn't even break anything! Alright, a tiny, hairline fracture of the nose, but I apologised.

The trouble is with Cassandra, you can't sit down and discuss problems that arise in our marriage in a mature and adult way. I just happen to point out that there's nothing for me to eat - again - and she says I'm caught in a time warp! 'This is not 1933, Rodney,' she says, 'and the sooner you realise that the sooner you'll stop being so bloody childish!'

At times like these I wondered how Rodney had ever qualified for a diploma in the Trotter Way to Romance.

It's at this point in the proceedings that Rodders would have done well to thumb through the Trotter Way to Romance, and stop at the section headed **WHEN NOT TO BRING UP THE SUBJECT OF OTHER WOMEN**. So here you are, Rodders, for the next time:

When not to bring up the subject of other women

1. Whenever you're trying to have a mature and adult discussion with the enemy about problems in your marriage, and
2. Pretty much the rest of the time, unless she's well out of the way and you're in a bar reminiscing about the old days with a few mates.

In other words, you *don't* wade straight in there with:

'Cassandra, if you could avert your gaze from the exotica of the banking world for just one minute, you would realise, as so many women in Peckham realise that there is nothing childish about Rodney Trotter! And believe me, they would appreciate having a young, successful and vibrant man like me around! What's more, they'd most probably do me a pie and chips if I fancied it!'

'Well,' she says, with that steely tone in her voice that she probably uses to give people a bollocking about their overdraft, 'why don't you go and find one of these women?'

Even now I reckon Rodders could have saved the day, if only he'd said something like: '*Bouillabaisse, ma cherie,* just my little joke!' Instead of which, he skidded past the point of no return and said:

'Alright , I will!'
'Well go on then!' she says.
'I will!' I say.
'And take a bottle of ketchup for your pie and chips!' she says.
And I do!

Keeping a sense of humour is vital

I don't know about you, but I reckon a bloke needs a sense of humour at a time like this. I certainly did when Rodders stormed back into the penthouse suite just as I was about to learn a bit more about Raquel's vital ballistics.

'Listen,' I said. 'Calm down, finish your drink, then I'll drive you home and we'll sort it all out.'

'You don't seem to understand!' he yelped. 'I'm not going back! Me and Cassandra are finished – for good!'

'Rodney, you'll have to at least talk to her sooner or later,' Raquel soothed. 'There'll be things to be discussed . . . '

'Yeah,' I said. 'Like who gets custody of Barbie and Ken!'

He didn't appreciate that at all.

'It's all a big joke to you, ain't it Del?'

I shook my head. 'I just think that you and Cassandra are both behaving like a couple of ten year-olds! You've only been married eighteen months and already you've broken up more times than JR and Sue Ellen!'

Making her jealous

I've got to tell you I don't recommend it at all. If you go this route without Del Trotter there to pick up the pieces.

'Course, that dipstick Mickey Pearce knew different. We'd all gone down the disco where Rodders had first pulled Cassandra and pocketed twenty nicker into the bargain. This time around he couldn't even get arrested – though the amount of time he spent with his mates Johnny Walker and Ron Bacardi, it wasn't for want of trying.

I was getting another couple of drinks for me and Raquel at the bar when I overheard Mickey giving Rodders the benefit of his lifetime's experience.

'What you've got to do is make Cassandra jealous.'

'Yeah!' Rodney said, with the enthusiasm of the truly legless. 'Why?'

'Make her think other women find you desirable.'

Rodney and his old mate Johnny Walker.

'Yeah!' Rodders little eyes lit up, even the red bits.

'Don't encourage Rodney to tell her lies!' Jevon chimed in.

'That's right!' Rodney said, nodding his head. 'What do you mean, lies?'

'Listen to me,' Mickey said. 'I always make a point of making women jealous.'

'The only time you ever made women jealous, Mickey, was the night you won the last house at bingo,' I said.

It was time to take Rodders aside. I'd begun to realise that something was really bothering him. That's how I came to give him the most important lesson in the book:

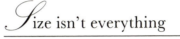

*S*ize isn't everything

It happened like this:

'You and Cassie split up eight days ago, bruv,' I said. 'It's time for you to go home.'

'But Del, her determination has made her so blinkered she doesn't notice all the beautiful things that are around her.'

'What, you?' I said.

'Well, if you like! The other month it was her birthday. So I bought her a pair of earrings and a Shergal Farkey LP.'

'A Shergal what?' I said.

'Shergal Farkey ... Fergal Sharkey, the singer ... '

'Oh, him,' I said.

'And a pair of earrings. They were nice earrings, but little. They were very *little* earrings. Nice, but ...'

'Little!' I said, catching his drift.

'Yes – little. Cassie looked at them and said: "Thank you Rodney. Aren't they little!"'

'No!'

'I suppose Mummy and Daddy used to buy her *big* presents! I wish I could meet another girl!'

Blimey, I thought. We had enough trouble steering him towards this one.

'In your present condition,' I said reassuringly, 'your best bet's to join a Lonely Kidneys Club!'

'I think married life's been a bit of a let down to Cassandra, but I don't care! I don't give a monkey's toss!' he said. Then the combination of booze and high octane emotion became too much for him. 'I love her Del!' he said, sobbing. He wasn't half making a mess of my jacket.

'Size ain't everything Rodders,' I said gently.

This didn't calm him down as much as I'd hoped. He went rigid and said: 'What do you mean, "size isn't everything"?'

'I'm talking about the earrings,' I said.

'Sod the earrings,' he said.

He walked away, his face like thunder, to go and find a little bloke to have a fight with.

If Rodney had managed to stay away from the Bacardi diet at any time over the next few days, he might have realised that he'd taken a seriously wrong turning. He'd spun off the Trotter Way to Romance and was heading straight down the path to destruction.

Things got so bad he'd even planned to take a bird called Tania to the movies.

'Tania ... ' I said. 'Tania? Not that old bow-wow from the exhaust centre?'

'She's not a bow-wow!'

'Do me a favour Rodney. It's like a Rottweiler with
112 a wig!'

'Del,' he said through clenched teeth, 'the Tania I'm talking about is very pretty.'

'Have you checked the hooter on it?' I said. 'Me and Boycie had a bet once whether it was real or she'd had silicone injections!'

'Have you actually spoken to this person?'

'I said good morning to her once, but she was busy gnawing a bone.'

Things went a bit ugly at this stage, and I'm not just talking about Tania. Raquel hadn't realised that I was busy saving Rodney's marriage and really got her wild up.

'You can be such a sexist Del!' she said. And that was just the beginning. She accused me of everything from pig ignorance to starting the Aids epidemic.

Rodney watched me getting it in the neck with glee. 'Get him on to politics, Raquel,' he said when she was in full flow. 'It'll blow your mind!'

Rekindling the flames of passion

It was some time before things quietened down enough for me to take the stupid little plonker aside and give him the Trotter patent remedy for getting the show back on the railway.

'Listen Rodney,' I said. 'One little row and you two think your marriage is dead. But it's not, bruv. You could rekindle the flame of passion. Take her a bunch of flowers and a bottle of champagne.'

'That's a bit corny, ain't it?' he said.

'No,' I said. 'That's what I'd do.'

'It wouldn't work, Del. She goes to evening school tonight. Nothing comes between her and her stupid, rotten career. Trying to rekindle the flame in my marriage is like giving the kiss of life to a rasher of bacon.'

'He who dares wins, Rodney,' I said. 'Just tell her you're sorry and then she'll say she's sorry as well. Before you know it you've made up, you're more in love than ever – *and* you might get a little bit! Everyone's a winner! *Tête de veau!*'

'Stuff it,' he said.

113

As soon as he'd gone I took a leaf out of my own book and called through to Raquel. 'Do you fancy popping out for a drink, sweetheart?'

'What, with a creep like you?' she said.

Women! What a life!

Then I had a terrible thought. Rodney was headed for the cinema right next door to Cassandra's evening class. He was taking Mickey Pearce's advice! It only needed Cassie to spot him and Tania in the queue for Rodders to crash and burn. I had to do something fast.

As it turned out, he'd listened to me after all. He cancelled Tania and presented Cass with the champagne and flowers as she got back to their flat that night. It should have worked a treat. And it would have if I hadn't nipped round first to warn her not to be upset if she saw him going to 'Honey I Shrunk the Kids' with some tart from the exhaust centre. But what can you do?

The love bug

They ain't got a clue about the way to run a successful romance, the kids today. Take Rodders – and I wish somebody would. He was so cut up about losing Cassandra he was beginning to get more and more confused. Confused as a newt, some nights.

'I've got a viral condition,' he announced as he plonked himself down at the breakfast table one morning after yet another night of doing Ninja Turtle imitations down the Nag's.

'Must have come on sudden, Rodders!' I said. 'You weren't feeling any pain at all last night!'

He said nothing.

'You looked in the mirror this morning?' I asked him. 'I tell you, Rodney, you are not the fairest in the land! You look like you've just come back from a Club 18–30 trip to Chernobyl!'

'Chernobyl's not too far from the truth,' he said. 'My love life has taken on a distinctly Russian ambience of late. Freezing bloody cold and the goods rarely turn up!'

'I was in the Soviet Union for a while,' piped Uncle Albert.

'They wouldn't let you into the Soviet Union,' I said to Rodney. 'Gawd, they wouldn't let you into the plumbers' union!'

'I was dry-docked in Murmansk for over a month,' Albert went on, full steam ahead. 'I met quite a few Russian girls – and I'm telling you they was hot stuff!'

'Oh leave off, Albert!' Rodney said.

'He could have a point,' I said. 'I mean, look at that love-bite on old Gorbachev's head!'

Still, joking apart, I couldn't let Rodney face his emotional destiny without the benefit of a few guidelines on the Trotter Way To Romance. I wasn't going to say '*bonjour*' to all the cheap printing deals he was putting my way, neither. I reckoned the best thing to do was give Alan a bell and see if we could meet and sort the whole thing out, relative to relative. While we were at it, I thought we might see about sharing his villa in Spain and all.

I got a peach dactari and a chipolata sandwich for myself, and a tomato juice for Alan. I'd forgotten he was on the wagon – I could see this was going to be a riot of an evening, about as much fun as a pub-crawl with Betty Ford.

'Poor Rodders,' I said. 'Most of the time he's feeling and looking horrible. I've told him, if he carries on much longer he'll be a dead ringer for Keith Richards. I mean, he looks like an extra from Halloween already!'

'What do you think's brought it about?' Alan said.

'Who knows? Sort of life he's been leading, I suppose. Late nights, booze, women, drugs.'

'*Rodney?*'

'Oh Rodney!' Blimey, I thought he meant Keith Richards. 'Well, it's obvious, ain't it?' I said. 'It's this thing between him and Cassandra.'

'So this row between them is more than just a lover's tiff then?' asked the unwitting supplier of half of Peckham's cut-price print.

'No, no,' I assured him, 'it's a storm in a teacup. 115

They've had a bit of a barney over something they can't even remember. Now pride's taken over.'

'I think I'd better have a word with Rodney,' Alan said. 'See if I can't find a few well-chosen words that might help ease them gently back together.'

What – like: Get back together with my daughter, you dozy little dipstick, or you're fired? I reckoned something along those lines might do the trick, but who am I to put words into other people's mouths?

Say it with daffodils

'I want my marriage to work,' Rodney said to me and Raquel later that night. 'I want me and Cass to go back to the way we used to be. If she wants to pursue her career and has to go to functions and seminars at the bank, then I don't mind. I really don't.'

'Well how about telling her that?' I said. '"*Revenons a nos moutons*" as the governor of the Bastille said whilst the flames licked around his old April.'

It's a good 'un, that, well worth bunging in the notebook. It's French for: 'I've got to do something, quick!'

'I've tried,' Rodders said, 'but we just row. I've apologised a thousand times for losing my temper and acting stupid. I've promised to be supportive and understanding. Just before she went to Spain I bought her a big bunch of flowers. Daffodils – Mum's favourites. But ... no good.'

'Yeah, it's a problem, Rodders,' I sympathised. 'Nowadays all you can do is keep your fingers crossed and hope for the best. Where'd you get them from?'

'What?'

'The daffodils,' I said.

'What's that got to do with it?' Raquel asked.

'Well, he said the flowers were no good,' I explained patiently. 'You should have asked me, Rodney. I know a bloke who'd do you a blinding bunch of daffs for a jacks – he's got a contact in the Gelderland.'

'The daffodils have got nothing to do with it!' Rodney shouted. 'I meant they didn't have the desired effect! She don't even like bloody daffs!'

'All right, keep your hair on!' I said. That's the trouble when you try to help someone out with a bit of emotional first aid. Their instinct is to hurt the one they love.

'What I'm trying to say is: I now realise what I might be losing. In Cassandra I found everything I'd been looking for. Before her I was, kind of, ricocheting through life like a rubber bullet, never quite sure what my future was. But Cassandra organised my life. She gave me something to aim for.'

'Which is very handy for a rubber bullet!' I said.

I think Rodney took my point on board, because cop a butcher's at this page I found in his diary:

She found our flat for us. For the first time in my life I had a real home. A nice home. With Cassandra I had a woman I loved. A woman who said she loved me... Now I'm half way between paradise and Nelson Mandela House.

I just want her to understand and believe that I mean what I say! I've tried everything in my power to convince her. I feel as if I've taken the mountain to Mohammed only to find he's already bloody got one!

RUBBER BULLET.

RUBBER BULLET.
HARD-HEADED, UNPREDICTABLE;
CHARGING AROUND, COLLIDING, KNOCKING
BIRDS
OUT;
DON'T KNOW WHERE IT IS AIMED,
AND IT DON'T
CARE...
RUBBER BULLET.

GUN.
HOT, EXPLOSIVE,
AIMING, FIRING, WOUNDING;
FINGER ON THE TRIGGER OF MY LIFE,
FEMME FATALE.

*H*alf way between paradise and Nelson Mandela House.

117

```
LYING BETWEEN THE HIMALAYAS OF MY LOVE

ONCE MORE AT BASE CAMP
IN THE HIMALAYAS OF LOVE,
AND YET I HOPE,
I GROPE,
I EXPLORE,
I PUSH DEEPER,
ONE LAST ASSAULT,
ONE FINAL THRUST,
BEFORE I SCALE THE PEAKS
AND PLANT MY FLAG,
THEN -
EVER REST!
```

Terminal, ain't it? I mean, is this a boy who needs help, or what?

'I've got an idea,' I said to him next morning.

I knew the manager of a luxury hotel not all that far from the airport. I used to go there sometimes myself in the mating season. A word from me could set Rodders up in the bestest suite in the hotel, the full works. So when Cassandra flew in from Spain – all suntanned and relaxed – he could be waiting with a lovely bouquet and the keys to the bridal suite. A mini-honeymoon – eighteen months after the first.

'Do you think it'll work?' he asked with a pathetic, desperate look in his eyes.

'Your best whistle, a splash of Brut,' I said. 'You'll be home and dry!'

Home and dry

Poor Rodders. There he was, sitting in the Nag's much later that evening, the man who thought he'd be enjoying the fruits of love and he'd ended up with a packet of pork scratchings. Not quite what I had in mind when I said home and dry. Not much to show for two hundred quid, neither.

I ordered a non-alcoholic lager to cheer him up, and a glass each of Mike's very finest cognac for Raquel and *moi*. I was celebrating. At that very moment, five hundred smackeroonies were winging their way towards me, tucked up safely in Boycie's pocket. Some villain had nicked his special high-tech satellite dish and Boycie had offered me five hundred quid to get it back. As luck would have it, I'd got hold of it via a business acquaintance of mine for fifty. You don't have to be that bird on Countdown to work out that I was four hundred and fifty quid better off.

'I had such high hopes for tonight,' Rodney reflected.

'I know,' I said. 'I could see it when you walked in.'

'Thanks for phoning the hotel and ordering that champagne on ice, Del,' he said.

'No problem, bruv,' I said. 'He gave you the best stuff, didn't he?'

'Oh yes, he charged me forty quid for it,' he said.

'Good,' I beamed. 'A lady like Cassandra only deserves the best. Bloody pity her plane was re-routed to Manchester, ain't it?'

Still, not to worry. As I pointed out, he could talk to her tomorrow, and anyway, she'd know he went to the airport to meet her, her Dad'd tell her. RULE NUMBER ONE OF THE TROTTER WAY TO ROMANCE: Always make a gesture. And that's just what Rodney had done.

At this point of the proceedings in came Peckham's answer to Cap'n Birds Eye, with a look on his face that said either he'd had too many rum and blacks, or he had something very important to tell us.

'Cassandra's up north,' he announced.

'I know she is,' Rodney said. 'But how do you?'

'She just phoned from Manchester Airport, wanted you to know she was safe and not to worry.'

'Where did you say Rodney was?' I asked.

'I said he was spending the night at some hotel,' Albert said. 'I couldn't remember its name so I gave her the phone number.'

'But you told her I'd gone to meet her at the airport?' Rodney said. Well, more sort of shrieked, really.

'Of course not!' said the old sea lord. 'It was supposed to be a surprise!'

119

Well done, Albert. Now she'd phone the hotel to discover that Rodney had booked the honeymoon suite in the name of Mr and Mrs Trotter ... She'd think he'd gone case-o with some tart for the night!

'I don't know how you're going to talk your way out of this one, Rodney,' I said sympathetically.

'If you hadn't suggested booking into a hotel for the night none of this would have happened!' he snapped.

'I didn't hear you object too much,' I said. 'It was your hormones that were on turbo, not mine!'

*Y*ou've got to be careful what you pick up

We went back to the flat but Rodney would have to sort his own problems out for a while – I had a few of my own. Boycie had come into the Nag's and announced that he'd got his satellite dish back. It hadn't been nicked after all – the engineers had taken it away while he was out. So what was that great big thing I had sitting out on my balcony? I finally tracked down the bloke who'd sold it to me in a bed and breakfast near Gatwick airport and got him on the blower.

'I just cannot get a picture from your satellite dish,' Raquel moaned as I picked up the receiver. 'Let's just unplug it and watch the ordinary telly.'

'Yeah, let's watch the news,' Rodney said. 'They might have another report on the ecological destruction of our planet – anything to cheer me up.'

I was still trying to get some sense out of the bloke at Gatwick when the news came on. Out of the corner of my eye I saw Moira Stewart and a picture of a satellite dish. I'll be honest with you, it looked dead familiar.

'The radar transmitter dish,' Moira said, 'similar to the one shown here, was stolen from Gatwick's main runway in the early hours of yesterday morning. The theft brought Gatwick airport to a standstill and has caused chaos throughout Europe and left thousands of returning holiday-makers stranded ... '

There was a bit of an awkward silence. For a moment, I didn't really know what to say.

Rodney looked at me.

So did Raquel. And her look did not exactly broadcast love, warmth, and the promise of a bit later on.

*B*eing given the heave-ho

I'm not one to dwell on failure, but you won't go far down the Trotter Way to Romance without tripping over it from time to time. It's always a choker, specially if you thought you was on a result – and it's vital you know how to pick yourself up and dust yourself off.

About five years ago I was given the old heave-ho by a rich bird I had very high hopes of. Her dad had left her a chain of launderettes in his will, and I'd just bought myself two tons of hookey Persil. It don't take a genius to work out that would have been a marriage made in heaven. For some strange reason she jacked me in shortly after I offered her the Persil at a knock-down price.

I went down the Nag's the next Saturday to drown my sorrows. It was Elvis night, starring the one and only Tony Angelino – a mate of Trig's from down the

*T*ony Angelino. When it comes to romance, I taught him everything he knows.

council depot. Five quid a head and I was miserable as sin. Nothing to do with the rich bird, mind.

I'd been to Lennie Morris's little kid's christening that afternoon. There was this marvellous atmosphere in Lennie's front room – his mum and dad were there, his wife and his little baby. I thought to myself, he's got all his family round him. A *real* family. And what did I have? Grandad and Rodney! Not much of a support system.

To cheer myself up, I got Tony to give the punters a burst of Old Shep – that's my most favourite song about a dog. It made me feel a whole bunch better, and I was just wiping a tear from my eye when I spotted a stunning sort on the other side of the bar.

'Excuse me gentlemen,' I said to Grandad and Rodney as I got to my feet. 'I feel a cultural encounter coming on.'

It turned out her name was Heather and she lived local. *And* she had class. My luck was definitely changing – especially when she let me drop her off back at her gaff in Brixton.

'I'm surprised I haven't seen you round before,' I said as I gunned the three-wheeler down the bus lane. 'I do a lot of business down this way.'

'What line are you in, exactly?' she asked. Just the sort of blunt approach us yuppies admire. The least I could do was repay her honesty in kind.

'I'm a sort of importer/exporter of quality merchandise,' I said. 'Antiques, that sort of thing. I tend to specialise in *Parisienne haute cuisine* fashion, superior *objets d'art* and modern works of art.'

'It sounds fascinating!'

'Oh yes!' I said, leaning closer. 'And I tell you what. If you're interested, I've got some very cheap washing powder.'

She showed me a picture of her three year old, Darren. He looked a lovely little nipper.

'Where's your husband these days?' I asked nonchalantly.

'I don't know,' she said, 'and I don't particularly care! He walked out of here one morning – said he

I've always known a thing or two about antiques. This piece is a Daulton. Noreen Daulton.

was popping down the Job Centre to sign on. That was eighteen months ago!'

'Well the way things are these days,' I said, 'he could still be queuing!'

'Do you know,' she said, 'when we got engaged he had a straight choice between going on holiday with some of his mates, or buying me an engagement ring.'

'Did he send you a postcard?'

'Like hell he did! Vic looked after number one. I don't think he was ever meant to be married. He couldn't accept responsibility. I used to say to him – you've got a baby now, Vic. Don't you think it's time you ... oh just listen to me! I'm sorry, Del, there's nothing worse than having your ear bent by somebody else's problems. I'm just tired.'

'Yeah, I'm due for an early start myself. I've got

to be in Eltham by seven to pick up a consignment of fire-damaged woks. I'll be finished by ten though. Didn't know if you fancied a day out somewhere? Spot of lunch?'

She'd love to. She'd see if she could get a baby-sitter.

'No,' I said, 'I meant you and the boy!'

'Are you sure? Most men don't want to know when they find you've got a baby.'

'I'm not most men, Heather,' I said. 'See you at eleven o'clock.'

We had a blinder of a day. My most favourite memory is her head resting on my shoulder as we stared dreamily up at a cloudless, star-filled sky. We embraced in a long, smouldering kiss that might have gone on for ever if a bloke hadn't grabbed the back of my collar and chucked us out. How was I supposed to know that snogging's out of order at the Planetarium?

A few weeks later, Rodney was on fine form as I got ready to rip the town up with my new bird. 'You must have spent a third of your life standing in front of mirrors!' he said. 'My earliest childhood recollection is of you standing in front of mirrors. Up until I was four I thought you were twins!'

'If you're trying to wind me up Rodney,' I said, 'forget it. It just won't work, bruv, because tonight is going to be a very happy, and a very special one for me.'

'What is it,' Grandad asked. 'Cubs' night?'

I slipped my suit jacket on. Their jibes were like water off a duck's back to me. I was a man with his sights set on an evening of romance with the woman he loved, who was the mother of a child he adored. For the first time in my life I was undaunted by the prospect of executive fatherhood.

'Well, how do I look?'

'You look like a second-hand car trader!' Rodney said.

I beamed with pride. Rodney can be a mouthy git most of the time. It's not often he choses to hand out compliments like that.

'I'm taking Heather for a meal she'll never forget,'

I said. 'Soft music, champagne, and the very finest of foods. I just hope she likes curry.'

Heather looked a million dollars as we walked arm in arm to our table at the Star of Bengal – and that was at the old exchange rate. I couldn't take my eyes off her.

'We'll have a chicken tikka, off the bone,' I said to the waiter, 'a mutton Madras, a brace of onion bhajees, four popadums, some nan bread and a couple of portions of rice.'

Heather was quietly impressed by my *l'etat c'est moi*.

'Yes sir. Which rice would you like?'

'You got any Uncle Ben's?'

'No sir. We have pilaw rice, basmati rice or plain white rice.'

'We'll have the pilaw,' I said. 'But don't forget to take the feathers out. And bring us a bottle of your finest champagne.'

'You're pushing the boat out, aren't you?' Heather smiled.

'I'm always like this when I have something to celebrate.'

'Oh yes, and what are we celebrating? You've sold all those woks?'

'No, I got a bit lumbered with them actually. I've started giving them away free with packets of Persil!'

'So what's the champagne in aid of?'

I produced the ring box and placed it on the table in front of her.

'It's Christmas!' I said.

'What is it?' She could hardly conceal her emotion.

'Open it and see!'

'It's lovely!'

'I got it off this mate of mine, Abdul. He gets discount from Hatton Garden!'

'Del, is this an engagement ring?'

'No, it's a set of socket spanners!' I laughed. 'Of course it's an engagement ring!'

She lowered her eyes. At first I reckoned she was a bit embarrassed by the size of my generosity. Then I twigged – she didn't like the ring ...

'I can change it if you like,' I said. 'I remember you

saying you liked solitaire diamonds – so I thought, I'll get her a whole cluster of them!'

'No, the ring's beautiful, Del.'

'So what's wrong?'

'It's Vic.'

'You got a blocked-up nose?'

'No! Vic my husband!'

'Oh? What about him?' Wherever this was leading, I didn't like it.

She took a deep breath and started talking. He'd written to her last week. She'd been trying to find the right moment to tell me. Seemed he was living in Southampton, had got himself a nice little flat. I was almost beginning to feel happy for the geezer.

'Del,' she said, biting her lip. 'he wants me and Darren to move down there with him – to try again, see if we can make it work this time.'

'You're not going to fall for that old pony are you?' I exploded. ' . . . Are you?'

'He's still my husband, Del,' she said. 'He's Darren's father! I owe it to him!'

'Don't give me that, Heather,' I said. 'That bloke couldn't give a monkey's about you and Darren. When the going got heavy what did big brave Vic do? He put on his hiking boots.'

'You don't know what he's like, Del!'

She was wrong. He was like my old man because that's exactly what he did eighteen years ago.

'But it wasn't his fault! He was unemployed – all he wanted was regular work. You've got no idea what that sort of pressure can do to a family! He's managed to get himself a job now in a department store.'

'Doing what?' I asked.

'He's a Father Christmas!'

'Oh, well that's a steady little number, ain't it?' I said. 'Uniform, luncheon vouchers and forty-eight weeks a year holiday!'

'Despite everything – I still love him!'

Yes, but what about me?

'I love you Del, but not in *that* way! I love you the way someone would love a . . . '

126   'A goldfish or a gerbil?'

'No! Like a brother! I feel for you the same way as you feel for Rodney.'

And I thought she liked me! 'You see Heather, I thought that you and me had ... well, an understanding!'

'Honestly Del, I never knew you felt that strongly! I mean, you never said anything.'

'I'm not a poet, Heather,' I said. 'I'm a businessman. I thought it was obvious the way I felt. I mean, what more could I have done?'

'If you'd have just given me ... well, a sign.'

'A sign? What did you want me to do – tie a yellow ribbon round the old oak tree?'

I was wasting my breath, and I knew it. She was leaving next Tuesday.

'Will you come round and say goodbye to Darren?' she asked.

I shook my head.

'He really took to you. You like kids don't you?'

'Yeah,' I said, 'I used to go to school with a whole lot of them.'

Heather handed me back the ring.

'It's a beautiful ring, Del. Thank you.'

'Normally I'd let you keep it,' I said. 'But I only got it on a week's approval.'

'I don't really feel hungry any more, Del,' she said. 'I think I'll go.'

I started to stand but she put out a hand to stop me.

'No, Del – I'll get a taxi.'

And those were the last words Heather ever spoke to me. She walked slowly towards the door, then stopped, turned, and looked at me. I looked at her. And then she was gone.

I sat down slowly, my head spinning with a thousand unanswered questions. I stared at the table for what seemed like an eternity. Then, at last, I made up my mind. I changed seats so that I was sitting where my beloved had been sitting. I picked up her fork, and tucked in. Well I mean, you can't waste a good mutton vindaloo, can you?

The importance of a good appetite

Since Eve handed Adam a beautiful shiny Cox's Orange Pippin and suggested he had a bit, food and romance have been intertwined. My Gran was a dead ringer for Eve in this respect, but then they was probably mates at school.

'You wouldn't remember when I married your Grandmother,' Grandad once said to me.

'No,' I replied.

'The first night we were in bed and – well you know Del!'

'What?' I said.

'Well, we were doing what you do when the lights are out!'

'You mean you were holding a seance?'

'No! You know what I mean! Anyway, right in the middle of . . . it . . . do you know what she said to me?'

I hardly dared think.

'She said: "What do you fancy for dinner tomorrow?"'

'What do you fancy for dinner!'

'Bad, ain't it?' he said.

'Never happened to David Niven!' I said. 'What did you say?'

'Steak and kidney pudding, I think!'

Ain't love wonderful! I don't mind how often your Mickey Pearces and your Jevons claim that five minutes' chat and a half of lager is all it takes, I'm here to tell you that at some point in the proceedings there's no substitute for a full stomach.

And I'm not talking about a spot of humpty dumpty and a bacon sandwich at the end of a busy working day. I'm talking about *real* romance. That's when you get a nice juicy steak and all the trimmings, washed down with a bottle of Blue Nun and a brandy and cream soda to follow. I don't need to tell you, it don't grow on trees. And if you've ever seen Rodney and his friends doing their Tarzan impressions, you'll know why.

Any amount of *haute couture* is wasted on a bird if you don't pay a bit of attention to the accessories. A table cloth, a flickering candle, a bottle of Beaujolais Nouveau '79, Mantovani on the stereo – if you're not on a result after that it ain't just your aftershave that's at fault.

'Course, achieving the right effect don't come easy. It takes flair, it takes meticulous planning and whether you're launching a stock-market flirtation or impressing a bird with a big helping of *courgettes nouvelle*, there are times when you just can't do it on your own. And that's often where your problems begin.

I once invited a sort all the way over from Canning Town for an intimate candlelit dinner. All I asked Grandad to do was put my box of wine in the fridge and my tub of neapolitan in the freezer. But oh no, the dozy old twonk had to get that arse about face. By nine o'clock that night all I had to offer her was a bowl of gunge and a Beaujolais lolly. Ruined everything!

Mind you, it could have been worse. I once found him in the kitchen trying to tune in to The Dukes of Hazard on the microwave oven.

Grandad had passed on by the time Raquel arrived on the scene. Raquel ... Oh Raquel! I never got through to her when she was in Addis Ababa, on account of being a guest of the Old Bill. By the time

I'd managed to convince them that Rodney had been the one who drove the van through a red light, she'd moved on.

But she never forgot me. I mean, not a lot of people do, but this was special. She was touring in My Fair Lady – Atlanta, New Orleans, Miami, – then suddenly she got what psychiatrists call an 'urge' to come back to me. Kevin Kostner, eat your heart out. He never even got the chance to do lunch with her. In no time at all she was staying in Rodders' old room and romance was in the air once more.

The thing of it is, romance in the air's dead cushty, so long as you're in a jumbo jet. On the whole, though, I prefer it on a decent pasture sprung mattress, and we was taking our time getting to that stage in the game. I thought dinner for two and a spot of *oeuf sur le plat* might speed things along. I asked her to do the cooking.

It went down a treat. I don't care what they say about La Gavroche, Le Scargot and all them posh restaurants where the waiters sing 'Just one cornetto' when you order pudding – there's no place quite like Nelson Mandela House with the lights turned down low.

'Mmm,' I said as we mopped up the main course, 'what a meal!' I gazed into her eyes and knew that the moment had arrived to try a little bit of French.

Trying a little bit of French

At some point along the Trotter Way to Romance, trying a little bit of French is absolutely *rien ne va plus*. It takes practice, obviously, but it knocks them bandy.

'*J'y suis, j'y reste,*' I began, 'as they say in Montpellier.'

Her eyes shone. 'Does that mean good?'

'Superb!' I said. 'Haven't eaten food this good since my old mum was alive. What is it again?'

'It's chicken!' she said, saucy mare.

'I know,' I said. 'I mean what's the dish called?'

'*Petto di pollo trifolati,*' she said. Even I had to give her nine out of ten for her accent.

*T*he moment arrives to try a little bit of French.

'Say what you like about the French,' I said, 'but they're magic with a saucepan and a bit of salt.'

'It's Italian,' she said, as if I didn't know!

'Yeah I know it's Italian,' I said. 'I was just saying that the French are good cooks as well.'

I raised my glass and gave her my bestest smile. 'To ... the future ... ' I said.

*M*aking your move

Then I reached over and ran my fingers lingeringly across the back of her hand. 'Raquel ...'

'Mmm,' she said.

'You've been here a couple of weeks or so now, and ... well ... you know how I feel about you ...'

'Do I?' she asked. 'You've never said.'

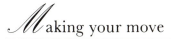

This is the toughest bit. Try one of the following. With Raquel, I tried them all:

a) 'I thought it was obvious ... '
b) 'I really like you ... '
c) 'I think you're really, you know ... '
d) 'You're incredibly ... '
e) 'You're special ... '

Then go for it:

'And ... you don't have to answer this right now, but I was wondering whether you would – '

'Course, if at that moment the main lights are switched on and a silly old bugger with a beard who looks like his head's been put on upside down comes crashing in, you're going to have to work hard to recreate the atmosphere.

'I've kept your dinner warm in the oven, Albert,' Raquel said. 'Is everything alright now?'

He ran his fingers nervously through his face fungus. 'I've cut the singed bits off.' He turned to me like it was my fault. 'You should never light a candle when you've got a man with a beard in the house!'

I thought about explaining that all this wasn't entirely for his benefit, but I realised it was a waste of breath.

'You shouldn't have leant across the table to reach the bread,' I said as he disappeared to eat in the kitchen. 'I've a good mind to report your beard to the council! If I hadn't been a bit lively with my Liebfraumilk we could have had a towering inferno on the rates.'

'Where were we?' Raquel said.

I moved smoothly over to the light switch and attempted to pick things up where we'd left off. I've had bigger challenges – shifting that shipment of fire-damaged woks was no picnic – but this was going to be the greatest comeback since Lazarus. I took her hand once more.

'You see, you're a woman ... '

'Thank you,' she said.

'And I'm a man ... '

Well, it worked alright for Peter Skeleton.

'And – let's be honest – No Man's an Island ... '

Little bit of Elvis Presley never does any harm, neither.

'Do you see what I'm getting at ... '

She gazed at me with indescribable yearning. 'No,' she said.

'Well, I don't want to rush things, but would you ... I mean would you ... '

The other thing you've got to watch out for at a time like this is your brother suddenly storming in and complaining that his wife's so keen on playing badminton with her banker friends that he's left her and decided to move back in with you.

'I have never been so insulted in my life!' he ranted.

'Sit down bruv,' I said, my evening shot to pieces worse than one of Albert's battleships. 'Let me have a try!'

Here endeth the lesson.

*G*etting it together

Getting it together ain't always a doddle, as my old sparring partner Sir John Harvey Oswald often says.

Course, the Del Trotters of this planet rarely go short of a bit, but you know, getting your card stamped by someone you really care for can take time. At the end of the day, it's all about instinct, and instinct can't be taught, even in the Trotter Way to Romance. You've either got it or you ain't.

Rodders, as ever, had a lot of difficulty getting this into his head. He couldn't understand that Raquel had been living with me for over two weeks without doing the bizzo.

'Just tell her that, like it or lump it, she's got to kip with you!' he said.

'Listen to me, Rodney,' I explained. 'Raquel is a lady. And when a lady is ready to ... well, when she's ready she'll let me know.'

'How,' he asked, always willing to kneel at the feet of the Master.

I hesitated. 'She'll give me a sign.'

'Like what?' he said.

'I don't know Rodney.' How could I describe that   133

uncanny seventh sense that only the true magician possesses?

'Maybe she'll put an announcement in the Sunday Sport,' he said.

As far as I was concerned, it was never in doubt. It was just a question of time, and the right combination of alcoholic beverages. But it's no use using the steam-roller approach, whatever Rodney says. You've got to make a bird feel protected, to feel safe from the terrors of the outside world. *Then* you jump her!

The first step is to find out what she's frightened of. My chance finally came down the disco. While Rodders and his mates were impressing nobody but each other, I was on a home run with Raquel.

'What are you frightened of?' I asked.

She smiled and brushed her fingers down my cheek. 'Shut up,' she said. 'You'll make me feel silly!'

'Go on,' I said, 'I promise I won't laugh.'

She hesitated. 'The dark.'

The dark! I snorted with laughter.

'What, even *now* you're afraid of the dark?'

She nodded. 'Yeah, sometimes I lay in bed and the dark seems ... well, it seems to be touching me ... Stupid, eh?'

This was the moment I'd been waiting for. It could have gone either way, but he who dares, wins.

'If you like ... ' I said, 'tonight, when you're in bed ... in the dark ... I'll hold your hand.'

I held my breath and all.

Raquel treated me to one of her most warmest smiles and said: 'OK. Thank you.'

I was in love for sure.

'Come on then,' I said. 'Drink up!'

She took my hand. 'Listen Del, my reputation in this area isn't as good as I'd like it to be. So please don't tell anyone about this ... about us ... '

Cor blimey! What sort of bloke did she think I was? The one, single unbreakable rule in The Trotter Way to Romance is that this kind of thing's private. It's just between the two of you.

As we made our way to the exit, we passed Rodders and his mates, still standing at the bar.

'You off?' he said, sharp as ever. 'I'll see you later.'

'Righto,' I said. 'And Rodney, there's no need to kip on the sofa tonight. You can have your old room back.'

I've had a few standing ovations in my time, but the applause from this lot was something else.

I suppose a little luck's out of the question

Fate is a fickle mistress, they say, and to a man of the world like myself that's a constant source of worry. I mean, some of the birds I've knocked around with don't even know the time of day, so you'd have to be a right dipstick to trust them with your entire destiny, wouldn't you? No, there's no doubt about it, when the chips are down you've sometimes got to give Mistress Fate a bit of a helping hand . . .

I was in bed one morning with Raquel, enjoying my darjeeling and jammy dodgers and thinking how cushty life was. Just about everything a man could ask for I had – a good woman, a thriving business empire, a beautiful home. Lovely jubbly! I've always put a lot of effort into making sure I get things just right, and as I looked around me I knew that I had succeeded.

*F*eathering a love nest

My bed has sidetables built into the modern swirling brass headboard.

The bedside table on my side contains the built-in controls for the stereophonic radio, the one on Raquel's the built-in controls for the hidden lighting.

The bed is covered with black satin sheets, and on top of these is a lovely tiger-skin bedcover – mock, of course, on account of I'm sensitive to Rodney's feelings on environmental issues.

On the walls, which I've papered with the most brightest paper that Fads has to offer, hangs a picture of a nude woman I saw in Boots (the picture, not the woman) and a painting of a Ferrari, done by Turner or Constable I'm told – one of them French impersonators anyway.

The two sidelights – and this shows how it's the little things that can make all the difference – hold small glass chandeliers.

On the pine and brass dressing table I got from Texas Homecare stand numerous bottles of after-shave and deodorant, the working-man's best friend. Brut, Blue Stratos, Old Spice – you've gotta go upmarket if you want to get up the right noses.

The white, Georgian-style MFI wardrobes complete the decor, giving the whole room that subtle ambience of early B&Q.

Lying next to me was the love of my life, Raquel. She was having lunch later that day with her show business agent. She was up for an audition – Rosalind in Shakespeare's As You Like It.

'I've never told anyone this before,' she said to me, 'but do you remember I was in America for a while? Well, while I was there they were putting on "Aida" at the Met. So I applied for a part in it. I didn't get it – there were union problems and I wasn't very good. But, for a while, my head was filled with big theatres. You know, New York, Broadway – all that! Stupid really . . . '

'No, no,' I said. 'You didn't get it but the thing is you had a go! Anyway, I reckon it could have been for the best.'

'How?' she asked.

'Well, "Aida At The Met"! I just couldn't see you playing a policewoman.'

When I said just about everything was perfect in my life, I forgot to mention Rodney: he was still staying with us. He knocked on the bedroom door.

'Am I interrupting something?' he called out.

'No,' I said.

'Oh well, better luck next time,' he chirped as he came in.

I thought it was time to subtly remind him of Cassandra's existence, sort of vaguely hint at his relationship with her, gently probe into his plans for repairing it.

'I'm going round your flat today to repair the front door you kicked in because Cassandra changed the locks,' I said. 'Have you spoken to her since she got back off holiday?'

'No,' he said defiantly.

'Why don't you ask to meet her?' Raquel tried. 'Talk things over quietly between yourselves?'

'If she wants to make the first move then fine,' said Peckham's answer to Conan the Barbarian. 'Other than that – nito!'

'But she's only just got back from Spain,' I said. 'Can I at least give her a message from you?'

'Yeah,' he moped, 'say *hasta la vesta.*'

'*Vesta?*' I said to Raquel when he'd gone. 'That's boil-in-the-bag curry, ain't it?'

Through the keyhole

'Thanks for everything, Del,' Cassandra said as I put my shoulder to the new front door I'd fitted for her. It seemed a bit on the big side for the doorframe, I must admit. Still, as my old Mum always said, if you've gotta have one, have a big one. The wood would shrink with time. A couple of weeks from now it would look like it was made-to-measure.

'You don't have to thank me,' I said. 'We're family, Cassandra. You're my sister-in-law.'

'Yeah. Don't know for how long though,' she said. She sounded sad, but I couldn't tell if that was because of the state of her marriage or because of the state of her new front door.

'You and Rodney still at battle stations, are you?' I said.

'Seems like it,' she sighed. 'We haven't spoken for ages.'

It was time, I reckoned, to give fickle old Mistress Fate's finger a bit of a leg-up.

'Well, I think Rodney's had a change of heart,' I said. 'We were having a chat earlier, and he said that he still loves you ... very deeply.'

'Rodney said that?' she said, her eyes burning into me.

'Oh yes,' I said. 'He asked me to ask you whether you'd be prepared to meet him tonight?'

'Where?' she asked. She was trying to sound cool but I knew better. Her body language said to me she was eager, and there's nothing I don't know about a woman's signals. The one and only time in my life I got it wrong was when I was fifteen and I thought the bird I was with was gagging for a snog. How was I to know she was chewing on a hot chip?

Anyway, I told her about the little restaurant over Wapping way. 'I've got the address here,' I said, pulling out a scrap of paper. 'That's not Rodney's writing,' she said.

'No, he told me the address and I wrote it down. What shall I tell him?'

'Yeah, all right then,' she said. 'I've got nothing better on.'

Lovely jubbly!

'But tell him not to think he can buy me a bottle of wine and then walk straight back into this flat!' she warned.

'He knows that, Cassandra,' I said. 'I think he wants to – you know – woo again. I'll tell him you'll be there, seven thirty?'

'Fine,' she said. 'But how am I going to get back into the flat tonight? I don't know if I'm strong enough to open the door.'

'No problem,' I nudged her in the ribs. 'Rodney'll be with you ... '

I despair about Rodney sometimes. You tell him his wife has told you she still loves him deeply and wants to have dinner with him and what does he do? He disbelieves you! Honestly, if he can't trust his own brother, who can he trust? I mean, just look what he wrote in his personal diary that evening:

Del reckons Cassandra has had a change of heart. What - as well as a change of door? I wish she'd go for the grand slam and have a change of bank. Anyway, she told Del she still loves me. Very deeply. Yeah, likely. Still, you never know. She's asked Del to ask me if I'd be prepared to meet her tonight. He shows me the address on a bit of paper.

'That's not Cassandra's writing,' I say.

'No,' he says, 'she told me the address and I wrote it down... What'd you reckon then?'

'Yeah, all right,' I say. 'I've got nothing else to do. But I hope she don't think she can buy me with a bottle of wine and walk back into my life!'

'No, no,' says Del.

He reckons she wants to - you know - woo, again.

'I've booked the ta...' he goes on. 'She's booked the table for seven thirty, so you'd better get a move on.'

'Yeah, I'll get showered,' I say casually. 'And · thanks, Del.'

'What are you thanking me for?' he says. 'I'm just the messenger.'

I feel - sort of - nervous, and I tell him so.

'What you got to be nervous about?' he asks. 'She's your wife.'

'Yeah,' I grin, 'just be myself, eh?'

'No,' says Del, 'try and make an impression.'

Old flames can make things hot

I was down the Nag's that night because Mike and Trigger wanted to buy one my national anthem door-bells. Rodney had offered to drop them off on his way out to see Cassandra, but like I said to him, this was one job I had to do myself.

'See, Rodders,' I explained, 'they don't know they want to buy them yet.'

The Nag's was the same as ever, apart from the raucous din coming from a loud-mouthed peroxide blonde in a corner.

'I thought you'd banned laughing in this pub?' I said to Mike.

'With that sort I have. The two blokes have been plying her with drinks since six o'clock. I think they're fed up with it now.'

One of the blokes came up to the bar.

'Would you call her a cab?' he said.

'Yeah,' said Mike, 'something like that.'

'No, no, would you phone for a mini-cab. The lady wants to go to Battersea.'

Lady? I'd heard more lady-like noises coming from an abattoir. She was in a disgusting state. How can a woman let herself get like that? I mean, how can a woman like that have any friends? Disgusting, ain't it?

I like a lady to act like a lady, like my Mum used to. She knew a thing or two about sophistication, did my Mum. She was the first woman in Peckham to smoke menthol cigarettes.

Anyway, I can't stand to see a woman staggering round a pub dropping crisps everywhere, and you should have seen the state of this one! I don't know how any bloke could admit to knowing someone like her, let alone being seen in her company.

'*Del!*' she called out to me.

I spun around on my stool just as she stumbled across the room and flung her arms round my neck.

'How are you, darling?' she said with her tongue in my ear.

'Oh triffic!' I lied. I didn't know her from Adam. Or Eve.

'How long's it been?' she asked.

'How long's what been?' I said, a bit indignant. I mean, I don't normally mind a bird giving in to her natural desires when she first sets eyes on me and

Clothes: The
Rodney Trotter
Way. The Albert
Trotter Way. The
Right Way.

coming straight out with a personal question or two,
but this old bag was so blousy she'd have had to go
on a diet to get in the Roly Polies.

'Since we last saw each other?' she leered.

'Have we met?' I asked.

I admit I have the occasional Gran Marnier and
Pepsi too many and can't always remember things the
next day, but this was stretching the imagination just
a bit too far.

'You don't remember me?' she persisted. 'Trudy!'

The penny dropped.

'Trudy? Were we engaged??'

'Yes!'

'Cor blimey!' I said. 'You've changed, sweetheart.'

'Ain't we all, love,' she sighed. 'Hang on, I'll just
get my drink.'

As she reeled back across the room, something told
me I'd have to be Houdini to get out of this one.

'I don't remember her amongst your fiancées,' said
Trig.

141

'Yeah,' I said, '1970. We were engaged for about a month.'

'So it was one of your longer engagements?'

'Yeah,' I grinned. 'We broke up after Rodney's pet mouse nested in one of her wigs.'

And now she was back.

For probably the first time in my life, I wished at that moment that I was in Rodders' shoes. Romantic riverside restaurant, a beautiful woman beside me, a bottle of champagne waiting in the back of the van. Cushty! I know the evening went well for him because I happened to look in his diary a couple of days later.

*B*ody language:
how to read a woman like a book

Cassandra and I take our seats at the restaurant. She's sun-tanned, but cool. I'm as pale as a filletted whiting, but I'm sweating. She looks beautiful. I look handsome, but only in certain lights. She looks depressingly non-commital. She says hello. We kiss politely.

Now I'd like you all to gather round and listen closely to what I'm going to say here, because what's sauce for his goose is sauce for your gander too.

First point I'd like to make is, when a bird looks non-commital, that's just body language for: 'You look amazing and I think I'd really like to stamp your card, but are you all that you seem? I'm holding back just a little bit as I have been disappointed before.'

You've got to learn to read the signs, see, those almost indetectable nuances of behaviour that tell you whether what you're on is a promise or a hiding to nothing.

142   I mean, how's she holding her wine glass, for

example? If she's got four fingers tightly clenched around the stem, what she's saying is: 'I'm trying to keep a grip on myself because I find you so attractive I can't wait for you to get me outside in the van.'

If, on the other hand, she's holding the stem between her thumb and two fingers in a widespread V, I think she's telling you you've got as much chance as Jackie Charlton has of winning Miss World.

How she holds her cigarette is important, too. If she cradles it lovingly right up against the V where her fingers join, and runs the tip of her tongue wildly round her parted lips before she inhales, then you've got a definite case on your hands of what leading psychologists call 'humpty dumpty'.

If she smokes with her hand sort of cupped in front of one of her lungs, that's a good sign, too – she's saying: 'Don't get many of these to the kilo, do you?'

'Course, if she just sneers and stubs the fag out on your hand, it don't take Clement Freud to tell you what she's saying!

So don't be put off by appearances – go for it! If a bird's looking a bit frosty you've got to make her thaw a bit. Get her to open up – go on, ask her something about herself ... Ask her how she managed to resist all that *paella* and *sangria*. Ask her if she's glad to be back at work. If you're totally stuck, you could even ask her if she missed you ...

'So how was Spain?' I ask.

Gordon Bennett! Not exactly open-ended, is it? Not exactly giving her room to manoeuvre, is he? I mean, what's she supposed to say to that – 'Oh, you know, okay?'

'Oh, you know, okay,' she says.

Well what did he expect, the plonker! She's a woman, ain't she? She's sitting there dying to talk to him about all her feelings and emotions and he goes and asks a

dipstick question like that. He'll be asking her how
the bloody car's running next!

'Good,' I say. 'Do anything interesting?'

Bit better. At least you didn't say 'any*one*'!

'Not really. There was just Mummy and I at the villa. To
be honest it was a bit boring.'

If you're ever in this situation, don't say it! Promise
me you won't say –

'I can imagine!'

He said it. Oh, nice one. I mean, RULE NUMBER ONE
OF THE TROTTER WAY TO ROMANCE has always been:
To get the evening really going with a swing, start by
having a pop at the bird's mother. Knocks them
bandy, that does!

'No, I don't mean being in your mother's company is boring!'
I say. I feel like I'm stuck in quicksand. 'I mean, she's
not a boring person. Would you like a glass of something?'

That's it, get a Caribbean Stallion down her! Nice
little thigh-tingler ...

She says she'll have the same as me.
'It's mineral water,' I say.
'Thats makes a nice change,' she says. 'I was told you'd
been drinking heavily.'
'Heavily! Silly!' I guffaw. 'I think your father was
exaggerating slightly, Cassandra.'
'Daddy didn't tell me,' she says, 'it was Del.'

It was for the best, believe me. I did it for him.

Thanks, Del! Whose side are you on anyway?
'Yeah, well, maybe I did go a bit overboard,' I say 'after-
you know - we left each other.'
'You mean you left me!' she says sharply.

Counterpunch, quick thrust and parry my son! It's the only answer.

'Same thing,' I say.

No it isn't.

'No it isn't!' she says. 'I didn't go anywhere, Roddy. I was
at the flat waiting for you. You just didn't come home!'
'Look, we came here to discuss things,' I say, 'not to argue!'

Smart move, that. Appeal to her better self.

'You started it!' she shouts.

'Course, you can't win them all.

'No I didn't!' I protest. 'I went home while you were on
holiday. I didn't know you'd put new locks on the door!'
'Yes, I should have told you,' she softens. 'But that was no
reason for you to kick it in!'
'I didn't kick it in.' I say, shoving an imaginary door with
my shoulder. 'I sort of ...that's all.'
'Why did you go back?'
'I wanted to surprise you.'
'You did surprise me! I didn't expect to come home and
find my husband had kicked the front door in!'

Take it from a pro, when you start going round in circles like this, it's time to get off. Break out a bit, try 145 a different tack. I know – tell her you kicked the door in because you wanted her desperately and your animal instincts got the better of you.

> 'Look,' I say, 'I've got as much right to enter that flat as you! We've got a joint mortgage, remember, from the bank!'

What's he trying to get her to do – stab him with the steak knife?

> 'And what about that girl you took out?'
> 'I didn't take any girl out!'

I give up.

> 'You asked a girl out!'
> 'That was just to make you jealous,' I explain. 'But it was a stupid idea and I never went through with it – although, at this moment in time, it strikes me as one of my better moves!'

Yes, well, I think that just about brings the proceedings to a close, maestro.

> 'Well this is obviously going to be a total waste of a good evening!' Cassandra says. 'Just think of all the more interesting things I could be doing – like washing my hair. I came here this evening hoping that you and I could find some common ground on which we could base our future! But it's just pointless! I'm glad I found out this early in our marriage what you're really like! Your drinking, your bouts of violence! God, I can just imagine my future with someone like you! You really are the silliest, pettiest, most childish person I've ever had the misfortune to marry.'
> 'You fancy me, don't you?' I grin.

I don't believe he said that!

'No I don't!' she says.

'Yes you do, you little flirt, you!'

'Oh shut up!'

'What I meant by 'surprising' you was, I wanted to be in our flat when you got back. Not just to say welcome back, but be living there! That's why I got so angry when I couldn't get in. What did you change the locks on the door for?'

'Because you walked out!'

'I know, but I only went to post a letter!'

'Oh, I hate you!' she laughs. 'I wanted this to be serious. I wanted to really tear into you!'

'Oh that's why you asked to meet me?'

'I ask to meet you! You must be joking! Roddy, you're the one who did the asking.'

Uh-uh, trouble ...

'No, Del came home and said you wanted to meet me. You even suggested this venue.'

'Rodney, Derek brought a message round from you. He said you wanted to meet me at this rest...'

Whoops.

'Del!' she exclaims.

'Yeah, Del! Git!'

'So, what do we do now?' she asks.

'Dunno... d'you fancy showing me your tan?'

'Yeah all right.'

She gives me the new key.

'I've got to go round to Mummy and Daddy's, I've left some of my stuff at their house.'

'You won't be too long, will you?'

'No, an hour or so. Do you remember your way home?'

It just goes to show, there are times when you make all the wrong moves, and yet just enough of The Trotter Way to Romance rubs off on you to leave you smelling like Yves St Dior.

147

Fateful Attraction

'**D**el!' Rodney beamed triumphantly, as he made his entrance at the Nag's. 'We're back together! Me and Cassy, we've made it up. I thought I'd just pop in and tell you that I won't be home tonight.'

'No, Rodney,' I said firmly, 'you *will* be home tonight.'

'Oh yeah, my real home!'

He handed back my key.

'Thanks for – you know – having me ... ' he said.

'Oh, it was a ... a pleasure, Rodders.' I hoped I sounded convincing – I didn't want to undermine his confidence at this stage of the game.

There wasn't time to say much more anyway because just then the mini-cab arrived for Trudy, and Rodney casually announced that he'd seen Raquel and Albert getting off the bus up the road. Blimey – action stations! Raquel mustn't see me with Trudy, she gets very jealous!

'Rodney,' I said, 'on your way out, escort this young lady to her cab, will you?'

'I'll see you, Del,' Trudy slurred. 'Do you come in this pub often?'

'No, it's the first time I've ever been in here,' I said.

'Ain't it Mike?'

Cor blimey! I thought as she staggered off supported by Rodney – talk about Fateful Attraction!

*N*ightmare on Peckham high street

'We've broken up,' Rodney announced as he came in the door about an hour later.

'Broken up?' I said. 'You've only been together ten minutes! What happened?'

What happened was, Cassandra saw him standing outside the Nag's Head with his arm around bloody Trudy!

'You had your arm around another woman!' Raquel said. 'Well no wonder she's thrown you out! It serves you right, doesn't it, Rodney?'

'Trudy was nothing to do with me,' he protested. 'She was ... '

I shot him a glance that said: if you want to stay living under this roof, Rodney Trotter, if you don't want me to say a word to Raquel, or Cassandra, or Cassandra's Mum and Dad, about your thing about uniforms, if you want to carry on benefiting from my advice and wisdom, and most of all, if you don't want a doughboy round the earhole, you won't say a word.

I think he got the gist: ' ... just a friend,' he said.

'Oh, just a friend, eh?' Raquel was back on the attack. 'How many times have I heard that! I've got no pity for you, in fact you disgust me! It wouldn't do you any harm to take a leaf out of Del's book.'

'Yeah,' I agreed, but I did feel a little panicky. I mean, how did Raquel know I was writing The Trotter Way to Romance?

A quiet night in

The next night all was cushty as I popped the cork from a bottle of my most favourite champers. It was definitely celebration time chez Trotter. Rodney's firm had won a big new contract with a mail order outfit and they'd all be eating turkey again next Christmas. And Raquel – well, she'd got the part I'd helped her audition for.

'There you go, darling,' I said, handing her some bubbly.

'Not for me, Del,' she said.

'But we're celebrating your good news,' I said.

'I've got this letter to read,' she said. 'It's all the detail of the play. I'd like to read it with a clear head. I'll see you in a little while.'

And with that, off she went to bed. I tell you, you can think you know a bird like the back of your hand, and then pow! she'll pull a stroke like that on you.

RULE NUMBER ONE OF THE TROTTER WAY TO ROMANCE: When you know for certain that a bird has only got two possible courses of action open to her, you can bet your bottom peseta she will take the third.

'What's up with her?' Albert asked, helping himself to the glass of champagne she'd refused.

'Dunno,' I said. 'She's been acting a bit off ever since she came out of that audition. Maybe it's being with that 'actors' crowd! Perhaps she feels she's a bit better than us now.'

'Raquel's not like that!' Rodney protested.

'You don't know, Rodney,' I said. 'A cravat and a codpiece can turn a girl's head.'

It's true. Everyone knows the only reason Michael Caine went into acting was to pull the birds. You won't have to go that far, of course, as long as you keep reading.

Raquel was sitting on the edge of the bed when I went in, just sort of staring at the floor. I knew at once that something was wrong; I could tell by the electricity. My new one hundred per cent pure crimplene pyjamas were crackling with static.

'You OK?' I asked.

'Yeah, fine.'

Even a less sensitive man than me, a bloke with emotional antennae nowhere near as well tuned in to women's needs and desires as Del Trotter's, could see that she wasn't really.

'Look sweetheart,' I said. 'If we've had a row will you at least tell me about it.'

'We haven't had a row,' she said. 'Everything's fine.'

No it wasn't. Ever since she met that Adrian and Jules and all them other theatricals at the audition, she'd been different towards me.

'What is it?' I asked. 'Maybe I'm not as good as your actor cronies, eh? Perhaps I embarrass you?'

'Don't be stupid, Del!' she said.

'I saw your face, Raquel,' I said. 'When Adrian talked to me about Hamlet and I said I preferred Castellas, I saw your face!'

I picked up the letter she'd been reading.

'So, when do you begin rehearsals?' I said, trying hard to change the subject.

'The tour doesn't start for another three months,' she said quietly.

'Oh well, gives you plenty of time to meet more of them intelligent, sensitive actor people, don't it?' I said.

She looked into my eyes and said: 'Derek, will you get it into your thick skull – I'm not trying to meet intelligent and sensitive people, I'm happy with *you!*'

Hang about, what did she mean – tour?

It was a nine week tour. I didn't know she had to go away!

'I thought it was just a play,' I said, 'you know, local ... Oh I see it all now. Your head's filled with big theatres again! Applause, applause, the show must go on!'

'We're not appearing in theatres,' she said. 'We're appearing in schools.'

'Schools?'

'Yes, schools. It's a co-project by the Education and Arts Councils. We're supposed to take Shakespeare to the inner cities. Imagine what it might have done for me.'

'Oh yeah. A few years from now you could have been a dinner lady,' I said.

'Don't become like the others, Del,' she said, fixing me with a sad, resigned stare. 'Putting down every little dream I have.'

'I'm not putting your dreams down, sweetheart,' I 151

said. 'You know I'd never do that. I don't want you to leave me. I'm frightened you won't come back ...'

'I'm not going anywhere, Del,' she said. 'I'm turning the offer down.'

'No, no,' I protested. 'You mustn't do that. It's a good opportunity, Raquel. I was just being selfish.'

'I can't do that tour, Del.'

'Why not?'

'Because I've read the play again and again and at no point does Shakespeare mention that Rosalind ... that Rosalind is pregnant.'

The rest, as they say, is history.

Still in a daze, I opened the bedroom door and went out into the hallway.

'Albert!' I shouted. 'Get out of bed, you lazy old sod, and open the biggest bottle of champagne you can find! Tonight we celebrate!'

'You're not angry?' Raquel said.

'Angry?' I said. 'I'm gonna be a Daddy! I want to phone everyone I know! I want to have a party – I want someone to put on a fireworks display for us!'

Rodney arrived on the scene in his dressing gown.

'What's all the fuss?' he asked.

'Rodney,' I said. 'Just stay where you are.'

Now Albert arrived at the bedroom door.

'What's happening?' he asked.

'Let me ask you two a question,' I said, pointing at Raquel. 'How many people can you see standing there?'

Albert and Rodney looked at each other.

'Well ... ' said Albert, 'one.'

I shook my head.

'I can see ... two!'

I smiled at Raquel and gave her a big hug.

'You know what this means, Albert?' said Rodney.

'No.'

'Well either Raquel's pregnant or Del's pissed!'

Pregnancy is a magical time. A time to sit and watch the woman you love bloom before your very eyes. A time to know that she is nurturing within her the heir to your business empire. A time to realise that you can

152

fancy what you like, but all you're getting is a nice cup of tea and a bacon sandwich.

But then again, I never underestimate the importance of diet.

$\mathscr{T}$he Peckham diet

Despite the joyous atmosphere within the Trotter penthouse, ever since Rodney went vegetarian he'd become a right miserable git. The fact is, you just can't do the bizzo in the boardroom or the bedroom without a regular intake of nice, greasy bacon sandwiches and a plate of chips on the side.

'A man needs a bit of fat and stodge to solid things up,' I explained to him. 'Any doctor'll tell you that. All that carrot and cabbage cobblers, no wonder you're depressed.'

He wasn't having any of it. 'I am depressed because 153

♥

of the state of my life at the moment. I've got this horrible feeling that if there is such a thing as reincarnation, knowing my luck I'll come back as me!'

I'm here to tell you that kind of talk is no use when it comes to pulling, and I'll give you a pound to a penny you don't hear it from anyone who's just polished off a decent bit of roast beef.

*S*omeone to lean on

It's at times like this that you need people. You feel like it's the end of the world, all you want is to be alone, but there's nothing like having a few mates

*T*here's nothing like having a few mates around . . .

around to offer advice and support. Luckily for Rodney, me, Mike and Trig was almost always there to pick up the pieces. The day Cassie gave him the elbow in the Hampton Court maze was no exception.

Trig told him the story of his cousin Cyril, and there are few better examples of how there's always someone there to help, no matter how bad things may look. Cyril was so far behind with his mortgage he was due to be thrown out on the street. He drove out to Beachy Head and parked about five foot from the edge of the cliff. He sat there for a couple of hours, his head resting on the steering wheel. People tried to talk him out of it, but he was too depressed to listen. But then, and this is what I mean about people, they had a whip round and got him his two hundred quid.

Rodney brightened for a moment. 'No?' he said. 'Who held the whip round?'

'All the passengers on his bus,' I said.

'Look, this is none of my business, Rodney, and you can tell me to keep my nose out if you like,' Mike said.

'Keep your nose out Mike,' Rodney said, his eyes never leaving the inside of his lager glass.

'I was married once and know exactly what you're going through,' Mike said with the voice of experience.

'You listen to the man, Rodney,' I said. 'His wife chucked him out *years* ago.'

'You don't want to take too much notice of things that are said in the heat of the argument.' Mike could have taken the words out of my mouth.

'She said that I'd always refused to adapt to married life,' Rodney complained. 'She said I wanted to carry on doing the same things that I'd always done ... '

I asked him what he'd said to that.

'I said I'm not discussing it anymore, I'm going down the Nag's Head.'

She also said he lacked ambition, and that's another load of rubbish. I mean, he must have taken that computer exam *five times* before I slipped the examiner a hundred and fifty quid to give him his diploma. Not many other students could claim that. They all passed first time. A thought struck me:

'That could be your silver lining, Rodders. Most 155

people come out of a broken marriage with a sense of failure. But you're used to it!'

Well, when it comes to romance, you've just got to keep looking on the bright side, and would you believe it, in Rodney's case it paid off.

If all else fails . . .

As so often in life, the answer to his problems lay in the TITCO stockroom. I'd taken delivery of a consignment of wigs, straight from a West End wig maker, via Mustapha the halal butcher's nephew. I picked them up for a quarter of their retail price, and I'd sold the lot to all the old tarts down the Nag's before I'd taken delivery. The only hitch was that they turned out to be men's wigs.

I'll be honest with you, I thought they was going to be git to shift at first. I mean, you can hardly go up to a bald bloke in a pub and ask him if he'd like one, can you? That's why I told Rodders to do it. Then I met the bloke who used to be Cassandra's boss at the bank, the one she asked round for a friendly dinner and Rodney smacked on the nose.

'I reckon we've had a right result with these syrups,' I announced when I got back home. 'I bumped into that Stephen down the market. He's got a pony-tail! I said to him: "Where did you get that Davy Crocket hat?" just to break the ice. And he said they was all the fashion up in the city! All the yuppies are wearing them.'

'But they look silly on men,' Albert said.

'Yes,' I said, 'but these days sophisticated, intelligent young men don't mind making prats of themselves. Because it attracts sophisticated, intelligent young ladies. He reckons the modern bird goes mad for them.'

I couldn't help noticing the gleam in Rodney's eye as he picked one out of the box.

'If you tried to sell one round here you'd end up taking a bite out of the kerb,' I said, 'but up in the city there's hordes of young career women getting the hots for those . . . '

Sure enough, when he left to see Cassie a bit later, he had one in his pocket.

The next time I saw him I knew he'd been on a result. It wasn't until I had another little butcher's at his diary that I found out how. He'd clipped on the pony-tail as he went up the stairs to their flat.

There I am flicking my head from side to side so she'd catch sight of the tail when what should she say?

'I saw Stephen today. He's been moved up to head office.'

'Cosmic.' A lot of other words spring to mind, but I don't use them.

'You know you used to call him a wally?'

That was one of them. 'Yeah,' I say.

'I think you were right,' she says.

This is a bit of a surprise. 'Was I?' I say.

'You'll never guess,' she says with that giggle that gives me goose bumps. 'He's only got one of those silly pony-tails!'

I manage to pull mine off before she sees it. Suppressing a roar of pain as it takes half my scalp with it. I fling the thing surreptitiously into the corner of the room.

It wasn't long before Cass caught sight of it and screamed. It really was Rodders' lucky night; she thought it was a mouse. He immediately recalled RULE NUMBER ONE OF THE TROTTER WAY TO ROMANCE: **SEIZE EVERY ADVANTAGE WITH BOTH HANDS** and everything else that's on offer. And that's just what he did.

'That's not a mouse,' I say. 'It's a rat!'
She watches in admiration as I wrestle with the pony-tail and finally, a little out of breath, overpower it.
'Don't worry,' I say, when she throws herself into my arms.
'I'm here...'

What followed is not suitable for a family readership, specially as Rodney does go on a bit.* Then again, it had been quite a while since he'd had a bit to go on.

The family way

I'm often asked whether my high pressure international business dealings will really leave me time to raise little Damien *and* keep the sparkle in my relationship with Raquel. I answer: Look at Jimmy Goldfield, Pete Walker, Norm Fowler – all of them top men in the marketplace. But what would they rather do than take a power breakfast or a weekend doing the business in the Big Apple? Stay at home and change the nappies, that's what.

As we got closer to D Day I even made a guest appearance at one of them anti-natal classes with Raquel. Amazing! It was full of pregnant women. Everywhere you turned there was ... lumps and ... things.

'Why did you have to go then?' Albert asked on my return.

I explained as patiently as I could. 'It's to get me ready for when we go into labour,' I said. 'They showed us films about how it all happens.'

'You've already got some of them in your cupboard,' he said.

* Copies of the full text is, however, available to advanced students of the Trotter Way to Romance who send a score and an SAE to 127 Nelson Mandela House, Nyere Estate, Peckham. Readies only please. Free inflatable doll for the first 48 applications received.

'Not them sort of films,' I said. I mean films about the birth and that. I tell you it's a miracle, a forty-two carrot miracle ... ' It made a lot of the blokes feel ill and all. Not me though. I used to run a jellied eel stall.

'So, what have you got to do ... you know ... when it happens?' he asked.

'Well, basically, be on my toes. Make sure the old Capri Ghia is running well and whip Raquel down to maternity a bit lively. But the most important thing a father does is showing the woman consideration and understanding, patience and love. I mean, as luck has it, I'm like that anyway. But it don't hurt to be reminded.'

'Where's Raquel now, then?' Albert said.

'Oh,' I said, 'the lifts ain't working again and she ain't as fast up them stairs as she used to be.'

I don't know whether it was the stairs or the excitement of being around the Trotters, but it seemed no time at all until Raquel was ready to pop. I assembled a small team of supporters and we took off in the Ghia.

We'd just got into the hospital delivery room when three people turned up in masks.

'Are those the specialists?' Albert asked.

'No,' Rodney said. 'It's most probably the Jesse James gang!'

One of the three was a bloke.

'Sorry John,' I said, barring his way. 'We're having a baby in here.'

'I know,' he said. 'That's why I'm here.'

This didn't sound at all good. 'What are you,' I said, 'some kind of pervo or something?'

It turned out he was the midwife. I still wasn't convinced we should let another bloke in on this, but Raquel was breathing a bit heavily by this stage and said she didn't care if he was a trained chimp. I warned him not to lay a finger on her.

Course, labour was no picnic at times, and very painful, specially when Raquel dug her nails into my hand. Still, another little snort of gas and air and I was right as rain.

My little miracle was born at 3.57 in the morning. When I stuck my head into the corridor and told them, Rodney immediately asked about the sex. He never thinks about anything else!

'Give her a chance!' I said. 'She's only just had a baby!'

Damien Trotter. He had a face, little eyes and a nose, little ears ... he won't be frightened to strip off in the shower room, neither. Ain't nature wonderful!

I took the new member of the TITCO board in my arms, knowing that I had discovered the secret of the universe. He's the most precious thing in all the world. Believe me, when you've got this far along the Trotter Way to Romance you'll realise that everything's been worthwhile. All them times you were stood up outside the cinema; all them times a bird's said: 'I love you Del, but not like *that* ...'

I was born for this moment. It has changed me forever. He is going to live all my dreams. Is this what Romance really means? You bet it is. I'll never forget the look Raquel gave me after she'd given birth, and the words she whispered in my ear:

'Don't you ever come near me again, Trotter!'

She didn't really mean that ... did she?

*I*n the end it's all a question of bottle.